NOT ANOTHER PARENTING BOOK

HOW TO CHALLENGE THE STATUS QUO, BREAK CYCLES, AND PARENT WITH CONNECTION, CALM & CONFIDENCE

InsideOut Publishing

Not Another Parenting Book

Published by the imprint InsideOut Publishing

Copyright © 2020 Michelle Catanach

All rights reserved. No part of this publication may be reproduced, stored in a retrieval system, or transmitted in any form or by any means, electronic, mechanical, photocopying, recording or otherwise, without the prior written permission from both the copyright owner and publisher.

ISBN (paperback): 978-1-9162504-8-2

Disclaimer:

All the information, techniques, skills, and concepts contained within this publication are of the nature of general comment only and are not in any way recommended as individual advice. The intent is to offer a variety of information to provide a wider range of choices now and in the future, recognising that we all have widely diverse circumstances and viewpoints. Should any reader choose to make use of the information contained herein, this is their decision and the author and publishers do not assume any responsibilities whatsoever under any condition or circumstances.

Contents

Introduction 1

Pace Yourself And Enjoy Parenting! *Dr. Ruth Oshikanlu MBE* 5

The Explosive Parent *Michelle Catanach* 25

The Perfect Parent Trap *Maria Alfieri* 45

Self- Compassion In The Heart Of Parenting *Maria Kefalogianni* 61

Nurturing The True Essence Of Your Child *Clare Ford* 83

Understanding The Impact Of Our Feelings On Our Approach To Parenting *Dave Knight* 97

Be You, Be Happy *Mark Newey* 119

Raising A Highly Sensitive Child *Jen Harrison* 139

Rewards, Consequences, And Praise: Why Are They Wolves In Sheep's Clothing? *Jane Evans* 167

How To Calm The Storm In An Angry Child *Rachel Devereux* 193

Your Teen Knows Best! *Cai Graham* 211

Self-Care for Parents and Children *Jessica Brittani* 235

Introduction

If you think this is just another 'how to' of parenting, think again.

Let's face it ... parenting can feel bloody hard at times! Perhaps there have been moments when you've wanted to walk out the door and never return. Maybe you've spent countless hours lying awake at night, your head spinning with anxieties and berating self-talk. Perhaps you wish you could take a magic pill to solve all of your parenting woes. No matter how many 'how tos' of parenting we may follow, we can feel like we're swimming against the tide, drowning in a sea of information, shame, and guilt as we desperately try to get this parenting thing right!

Children are not robots (and neither are you). There is no one-size-fits-all approach to raising unique souls in deeply complex human bodies. And frankly, much of the mainstream advice and strategies from reputable sources only serve to widen the disconnection between you and your child, leaving you spiralling deeper into shame and that oh-too-familiar guilt.

INTRODUCTION

In *Not Another Parenting Book,* 12 voices from a range of backgrounds and professions (psychotherapy, teaching, nursing, and healing, among others) share their insight, expertise, and lived experience to help you self-interrogate, challenge the status quo, and adapt to a new way of parenting – one that puts connection, compassion, and intuition at its core.

This book won't patronise or shame you, or tell you how much you're failing. But it may wake you up to a new perspective and approach, with implementable ideas that you can try and test with you and your children.

Not Another Parenting Book puts you and your emotional wellbeing, trauma, and experiences at the forefront – because parenting is an inside-out experience. The more we can heal (or even accept) our past and wounds, the more we are able to parent from a place of compassion and connection, firstly with ourselves, and then with our children.

It is our intention to bring you to a deeper level of self-awareness and understanding, not shame, though feelings of shame and guilt may arise as you read through these pages. If you find yourself feeling emotionally triggered, we encourage you to sit with the discomfort of those feelings, knowing that in those moments, you are safe, and being called to bring your attention to those emotions. Allowing ourselves to feel our feelings is a huge part of the healing process!

So, go and grab a cuppa and a quiet space, and allow plenty of time for pause and reflection as you venture through this book.

PACE Yourself and Enjoy Parenting!

By Dr Ruth Oshikanlu MBE

'Be the kind of parent you want to parent you.'

~ Ruth Oshikanlu

When one becomes a parent, one wishes their child came with an instructional manual. There are numerous parenting books, magazines, blogs and, of course, Dr Google! Family, friends, and professionals also give advice, a lot of it unsolicited and contradictory. This can leave parents feeling confused. How then can one start to navigate this journey of parenting?

I feel very privileged to have worked in the field of parenting for over twenty-five years as a midwife, health visitor, and pregnancy mindset expert. Having supported thousands of parents, from before conception, through labour, childbirth and beyond, one thing has emerged: most parents want to parent well … and enjoy it!

But what exactly is parenting?

Making lots of mistakes while trying to grow and raise another human being! Yes, I've said it! You *will* fail plenty. So, ditch the guilt! Making mistakes while parenting does not make you a bad parent! It is how we learn to parent. We learn first how not to parent, before we learn how to do it. But we strive to parent with love and empathy, and that is how we and our children learn and grow.

Throughout my professional career and my personal experience as a single mum, I have learned that, to enjoy parenting, just PACE yourself!

P for Preparation

When does parenting start?

I believe it starts before conception. Many of us give much more thought to buying or building a house than we spend in growing and raising our children. A strong house requires a strong foundation and takes a great deal of investment in time and resources to build. One cannot rush the construction of a foundation if one wants a strong building. Before one commences construction, a lot of planning and preparation is dedicated to what the building may look like. Time and effort are spent drawing plans and, eventually, digging deep into the ground to build a strong foundation.

Are you planning to raise a happy human being? If it's a 'yes', it's important that you start *before* the start, i.e. before conception. I learned this the hard way when I became a parent. I did not plan to become a parent and thus struggled when I realised I was becoming one. They say: *proper preparation prevents poor performance.* This was a mantra I was raised with. I was a good planner and loved taking action and seeing results. Yet, I was so ill-prepared for parenting. This was despite being a nurse and midwife. I had supported many people to become parents. When it was my turn, I did not feel ready! I believe it was because I failed to prepare, not just physically, but emotionally, mentally, and spiritually too.

As a pregnancy mindset expert, I support women and their partners to prepare for pregnancy. Many of my clients have had a previous pregnancy loss or assisted conception. I support them to prepare their body, mind, and spirit to become parents. Many prospective parents focus on physical preparation. They will eat a balanced diet, take nutritional supplements, regularly exercise, and ensure they get enough sleep, but often neglect preparing emotionally, mentally, and spiritually.

How can you prepare for parenting in a holistic way?

Prepare to receive. Many who have difficulties conceiving may view conception as an achievement. However, conception is not an achievement, but receiving of a new life. Therefore, allow yourself to receive the new life that will grow in you. Nourish yourself emotionally and mentally. Look inside you and imagine being your baby in your womb; visualise what you will want for your unborn child. Be mindful of listening to other women's pregnancy and birth stories, especially if they are negative. Each person and pregnancy is unique. Thus, envision the outcome you want – a healthy body that will grow a healthy baby; and a healthy mind that will handle whatever parenting experience you may face. It is essential that you trust your body and your mind. Be mindful of how you talk to yourself. Be your best friend and be kind to yourself. Make yourself your priority and love yourself. When love flows through you, beautiful hormones are released within your body that create a sense of pleasure, wellbeing, and security. And remember that you are never alone! Hence, start preparing your village, because it takes a village to raise a parent that will raise a child.

The first 1001 days - pregnancy and the first two years of life - are the foundation of life and are described as *The 1001 Critical Days*. They are crucial because it is when the building blocks of life are laid. Thus, it is essential that your child's environment and experience, both inside and outside the womb, are pleasurable and nurturing. I often use the analogy of baking a cake. To bake a great cake, one sources the best ingredients, follows the instructions to mix the ingredients and bake the cake, and then it is crucial to get the oven temperature right. If the oven temperature gets too high, the cake burns! Thus, it is important to ensure that you limit the amount of stress you experience in pregnancy, as it can affect your baby's experience in the womb. While some stress is fine in pregnancy, high levels of stress can create health problems, adversely affect the baby's development in the womb, and can lead to premature labour and birth.

Another thing that I have observed in my career is this: hurt people, hurt people! Hence, it is imperative that you process any unresolved trauma you may have experienced in your life. Trauma that is not transformed will be transmitted. Many may argue that they have been hurt but do not or have not hurt others. However, many hurt themselves because they are hurt. They numb their emotional pain with unhealthy behaviours such as overeating, not having healthy boundaries, use of substances, or other forms of self-harm. And by extension, the children they carry within them get hurt. Left unresolved, this trauma can surface in childbirth or in the postnatal period. Therefore, seek help to process any experiences in your life that may have wounded your soul.

Even with the best preparation, not everything will go to plan. Be flexible! Plans are great when they are not rigid. Be malleable as a parent. Allow your child to bring the best out of you as you get shaped as a parent and develop your parenting muscles.

A for Approach

The approach you take to parenting matters. Approach parenting with a willingness to learn. Part of learning involves unlearning some things we already know. Often, parenting is passed down from generation to generation. We tend to parent the way we were parented and may not recognise that some of the ways we were raised may not be healthy. As a child, I was raised with a tough love approach and was physically chastised as it was culturally acceptable. I was often told that children are to be seen and not heard. However, when I became a parent, I decided to ditch these approaches and adopted attachment parenting. I learned the importance of attachment and bonding and the role love plays in growing a baby's brain and fostering mental health. Love helps a baby thrive. I decided to love my baby abundantly. I encourage you to do the same.

One's mindset also matters. As a health visitor, I see many women doubt their parenting ability which affects their confidence. Many parents spend so much time striving for perfection which is unachievable. I am yet to see anyone who thinks that their parents are perfect. As children, we know first-hand our parents' numerous flaws. Despite this, many of us believe we had the best parents. Thus, ditch perfection and enjoy being a *good enough* parent. That is all your child needs from you. Keep learning and growing. You will fail many times. Embrace failure! Learn from your mistakes and grow from them.

Another thing that robs many parents of enjoying their role is comparison. Comparison is the thief of joy! You and your child are UNIQUE! Imagine parenting your child as a voyage that you are both going on. Plan to have lots of fun and enjoy it. Each child is different. Thus, each parenting journey is different. Avoid comparing your children. Even identical twins are each unique, each baby having their personality, likes, and dislikes. Enlist the help of your child. Your child is an active partner in the parenting journey.

A crucial thing I have learned as a midwife is that we focus on birthing babies, and often neglect birthing mothers.

Matrescence is the transition into motherhood. This period is like adolescence and a woman may experience hormone surges, body changes, and identity and relationship shifts as she grows as a mother. When a woman is becoming a mother, she often revisits the way she was mothered. If this was not positive, it may affect how she mothers. A mother may grieve the loss of what she never had and may use this experience to create a better experience for her child. She must also learn to manage all her social roles alongside parenting. If this is not managed properly, it may lead to fractures in her other social relationships. Cognitive restructuring can help one change negative thinking and adopt a more positive frame of mind. I encourage prospective or new parents to make time to look for the positives in their situation and balance the parenthood gains with parenthood losses. Look for evidence to counter the way you are thinking. By changing the way you think, you will change the way you feel and act.

C for Connection

Are you a connected parent?

To connect with anyone, you must learn to connect with

yourself first. As humans, we need to be grounded with ourselves before we can have healthy relationships with others. You can achieve this by making time regularly to connect with how you are feeling. Are there valid reasons for feeling the way you feel? If there are, then allow yourself to feel them. Feelings are meant to be felt. Therefore, try not to suppress them. Just like a river flows as we stand by the riverbank, our feelings will move through us and pass us by. Acknowledge your feelings by identifying and describing them. Make time for yourself and enjoy the time you spend alone. Engage in activities that re-energise and refresh you. Make it a daily practise, no matter how short the time you allocate to self-care. What matters is the consistency.

Once you are connected with yourself, make an effort to strengthen your bond with the significant people in your life such as your partner, family, and friends. Communicate with all your senses. Do things that will grow your relationship. It is important to nurture your village, in order for them to nurture you.

It is also vital to connect with your child right from the start of your relationship - in the womb. I learned the importance of this when I was pregnant. When I was 21 weeks pregnant, I went into labour prematurely and had to spend the rest of my pregnancy in hospital. Terrified I may lose my baby, I connected with him. I named him and started talking to him while he was still inside me. I used his name every time I spoke with him and waited for his response. I thanked him for remaining inside me every day I remained pregnant. I employed touch as I played music to him and watched his response and, before long, I was able to discern what kind of music he liked. This became my routine for the rest of my pregnancy, and I continued it after he was born. When it was time for him to be born, I had a long labour. After 21 hours in active labour, the obstetrician was concerned that my baby was getting distressed and advised me that I may require an assisted birth. In that instant, I spoke to my son, beseeching him to come out as I did not want a caesarean-section. To my surprise, he turned in my belly and was born naturally, 30 minutes later. Even though we were separated after birth for a few days (because he required admission to the Neonatal Intensive Care Unit), we continued to strengthen our bond once he was discharged. I liken it to having an online relationship with an individual. Even though you do not physically see them, you can form a relationship with them through regular communication, which then continues to grow when you get to meet them in person. My son is now a teenager, and I continue to grow my connection with myself and with him.

E for Embrace

I have learned to grow as a parent by embracing every experience I undergo, the good and the not-so-good. I believe that there is a lesson in everything I go through. I find I actually learn more when things do not go to plan. I have learned to immerse myself in my role as a parent. Although I am a sole parent, I call myself a soul parent, and parent with my heart, mind, and spirit. I focus on *being* more than doing. Whenever I face a situation, I ask myself: who am I being? What outcome do I want? How am I going to respond to get the outcome I want?

I have learned to ditch expectations and go with the flow. I view every day as an opportunity to create a beautiful experience with my son. My son and I are partners in parenting and I work with him to co-design our journey. I continue to learn to tune in to his needs so that I can meet them and regularly ask for feedback. Whatever the feedback is, I respect it because it is his experience of him being parented by me. I also regularly ask how I can improve. My son and I are a dyad that started our relationship in pregnancy. I liken it to a dance partnership. Each dance partner supports the other and regularly practises to improve.

Lastly, I have learned to accept my role as a parent and focus on the things I *can* control: my thoughts, feelings, and actions. I cannot control my child. As such, I do not even try. I just continue to PACE myself and enjoy parenting. I encourage you to do the same.

Are you ready to enjoy parenting?

Then PACE yourself!

Every situation you face as a parent, ask yourself:

P - How can I best **prepare** for the parenting experience?

A - What is the best **approach** to take?

C - How can I remain **connected** with myself, significant others, and my child?

E - What can I do to **embrace** the parenting experience?

Parenting is a journey and your child is an active partner in it. As you learn to PACE yourself, endeavour to ensure that your child is keeping PACE with you. Start before the start of life, and build a strong foundation that will enable your child to withstand life's storms. Trust your instincts and that of your child. Learn and grow with your child, and enjoy every step of the way. As you do, use your child as a mirror. Be the kind of parent you want as a parent. Be consistent and persistent. You will make many mistakes. Embrace them! There is no such thing as a perfect parent! But you *can* be a happy parent! And the happiest children are raised by happy parents. PACE yourself and enjoy parenting.

Let's Reflect

To enjoy parenting, PACE yourself!

Parenting is about making lots of mistakes while trying to grow and raise another human being! You *will* fail plenty. So, ditch the guilt! Making mistakes doesn't make you a bad parent - it's how you learn to parent.

Ditch perfection and enjoy being a *good enough* parent. That is all your child needs from you. Keep learning and growing.

Comparison is the thief of joy!

Embrace every experience - the good and not-so-good. There is a lesson in everything you go through.

About the Author

Dr Ruth Oshikanlu MBE is a multi-award-winning nurse, midwife and health visitor. A nurse entrepreneur, consultant, leader and parenting expert, she is passionate about supporting vulnerable children and their families to reduce health inequalities and improve their life outcomes. Her previous roles include: HIV specialist midwife, Family Nurse at one of the first pilot sites of The Family Nurse Partnership (an intensive home-visiting parenting programme for vulnerable families), and Nurse Leader of The Lewisham Young People's Health and Wellbeing Service for children aged 10-19 years.

Ruth is the author of *Tune In To Your Baby: Because Babies Don't Come with an Instruction Manual*. Having had a very challenging pregnancy, almost losing her baby in pregnancy, Ruth has developed a service for anxious pregnant women who have had previous pregnancy loss or have had assisted conception. Ruth is a parenting expert where she shares her expertise with pregnant women and new parents to enable them to parent in a more holistic way from conception through to toddlerhood. She helps parents learn to 'tune in' to their babies to create a deeper understanding and connection with their babies which promotes their neurological development, maternal and infant mental health.

Ruth has a passion for working with marginalised communities and has been involved with delivering numerous projects to meet the needs of vulnerable and socially excluded groups. She is a member of the Chief Nursing Officer Black and Minority Ethnic (CNO BME) Advisory Group and uses this role to advise and provide guidance on the issues facing patients and staff from minority ethnic groups. Ruth was a member of the Department of Health/Public Health England Task and Finish Group that worked to develop the recent Female Genital Mutilation (FGM) summary and key themes pathway.

Ruth is the expert blogger for The Nursing in Practice Baby Care Resource Centre which shares the latest news and clinical developments in paediatric nursing, health promotion and public health with the aim of supporting new parents and young children. She has written blogs on topics ranging from immunisation, effects on passive smoking on babies and FGM.

Ruth is a Queen's Nurse, Fellow of The Institute of Health Visiting, Royal College of Nursing, Royal Society of Arts and a Churchill Fellow. Ruth is the recipient of several national healthcare and business awards. She was named on The HSJ BME Pioneers 2014 List and The Nursing Times Leaders 2015 List. Ruth received The Queen's Nursing Institute's Queen Elizabeth The Queen Mother Award for Outstanding Service to Community Nursing in 2014 and was appointed a Member of the Order of the British Empire (MBE) in the New Year 2019 Honours List for being an Ambassador for the Health Visiting Profession and for services to Community Nursing, Children and Families. She was also conferred with an honorary doctorate degree from London South Bank University. Ruth is a regular columnist and has published several feature articles in numerous national nursing and healthcare journals. She has a passion for seeking out innovative individuals like herself and fulfils this by volunteering her time and expertise as a judge on different nursing, healthcare and business awards. In 2019, Ruth was awarded a Winston Churchill travel scholarship to investigate support for young people with adverse childhood experiences. At the start of 2020, The Year of The Nurse and Midwife, she received a Florence Nightingale Senior Leaders Scholarship and will be working to reduce the disparity in deaths of Black and Asian women in pregnancy and the perinatal period. In May 2020, Ruth was one of the 21 Churchill Fellows that was awarded funds by The Winston Churchill Memorial Trust (WCMT) to combat the effects of COVID-19 in healthcare and many other areas of UK life. Ruth's project focuses on the provision of culturally-sensitive psychological support to frontline BAME health and social care staff. Ruth is a Youth Mental Health First Aid Instructor. In her own time Ruth also volunteers as a coach/mentor for young girls with low-self-esteem. She has been able to achieve all she has despite being a single parent to a 15-year-old boy.

Connect with Ruth:

Website: www.tuneintoyourbaby.com
Email: ruth@tuneintoyourbaby.com
Facebook: www.facebook.com/tuneintoyourbaby
Instagram: @ruthoshikanlu

The Explosive Parent

By Michelle Catanach

'Freedom is not worth having if it does not include the freedom to make mistakes.'

~ Mahatma Gandhi

The time I saw terror in my daughter's eyes was the time I woke up. I won't pretend that I'm now so enlightened that those shameful parenting moments no longer happen. But I will say that it awakened me to the damage we irrevocably cause our children, even with the best of intentions, when we don't examine and heal the wounds and unresolved trauma we received from our own childhood and adolescence.

I remember the time well. Ronnie was 6-weeks old, and suddenly his arrival hit Emilia, then aged three, like a juggernaut. I was far from empathetic, expecting her to just 'get on with it' and accept her new baby brother, when only a short time before she'd been the centre of my world. Her behaviour deteriorated, and my egoic need to prove myself as being a 'good' parent who had it all under control - when I clearly didn't - was triggered.

Then she hit me. And I saw red. And, while I never hit her back, I grabbed her (forcefully), screamed in her face, then carried her over my shoulder up two flights of stairs, before dropping her on her bed, like I was discarding an unwanted toy.

As she stood there, sobbing and confused, pleading with me with her eyes not to hurt her, that's when I saw it. Pure terror.

I'd frightened her. She was scared of *me*. The one person who was supposed to protect her had left her physically and emotionally vulnerable and unsafe.

And at that moment I saw my own inner child, the part of me who wanted nothing but love, affection, and to feel safe, but who felt abandoned, betrayed, scared, rejected, and unloved. I remembered all those times in my own life when I'd felt that way, throughout my childhood, adolescence, and even early adulthood - memories that were buried so deep but never forgotten - and here I was allowing this vicious abuse cycle to continue.

Nothing prepares you for becoming a parent. Many of us have a romantic notion of what it will be like, a fantasy that we soon find rarely matches reality. I'm not suggesting that we shouldn't have children, and I'm certainly not demonising them. Kids are the most joyful and precious beings. We can learn so much from their authenticity, their aptitude to love unconditionally, and their presence. But what no one tells you is how emotionally triggering parenting can be, how children are often a mirror for our shadow, and how long-forgotten wounds creep to the surface before cracking wide open for the world to see. We feel vulnerable and exposed, masking the unwanted parts of ourselves to keep up the pretence that we've got it all figured out because, God forbid, anyone knew the truth.

Then we react to those wounds, that were never ours to begin with, inherited from a long lineage of wounded adults before us. But by default of being a child, we took them on, the baggage getting heavier as we grew into adults before offloading onto our own children. And so the cycle continues.

Learning to Abuse

Children learn about relationships first by how they are treated, and second by what they observe in their environment. 'Do as I say not as I do' is an adage that has never rung true. Treat a child respectfully, and they will know what respect feels like, and grow up emulating respect towards others. Treat a child with kindness, then they will *know* kindness, and will treat others with the same kindness that they themselves received. Bully, coerce, manipulate, dismiss, gaslight, disrespect and use power 'over' to control a child and they'll learn fear; they'll learn that they don't matter, or that it's okay to treat others as they have been treated. And if we're honest, that's what many of us do. So often we hold our children to a much higher standard than we can uphold for ourselves, expecting them to behave mature, rational, respectful, and kind, while we're unable to model those same behaviours.

I've said things and then, on reflection, realised how abusive those things were. I've emotionally pushed my kids away when what they needed was connection. I'm certainly not claiming to be a perfect parent - neither do I aspire to be - and neither am I sat here feeling sorry for myself and seeking reassurance and validation that 'I'm doing my best' and 'I'm a good mum'. Because at times I'm not. And frankly, at times I am so physically and emotionally depleted that I have nothing left in the tank to parent as my best self. It's in those moments that I dissociate, retreat into myself, and want to run away.

We all have regretful parenting moments and we need to take responsibility for them instead of looking outwards for someone to blame or seeking validation that we're 'not a bad person really'. The fact is, the victim-perpetrator dynamic that is entrenched in society has played out for centuries, and most of us have played both roles, including me. Furthermore, we don't need to be abusing our children for those dynamics to be present.

So many of us fall into feeling parent shamed when we're called out for our behaviour when what we're experiencing is guilt, guilt because we know in our heart that we've behaved in a way that is harmful. It's time to take ownership of our guilt and use it to effect positive change. Feeling guilty for times past when you didn't know better is futile; that kind of guilt only serves to shackle you to the past and create a barrier to moving forwards. But when you know better, you do better. It's a conscious choice. We *all* make mistakes, and with awareness (and self-compassion), we can learn and grow from those moments.

Children are very forgiving, and it's something we should never take for granted. They need to know that *yes*, we're human and we make mistakes, *yes* we can show empathy and compassion and recognise the pain that underlies the behaviour of others AND they need to know that they do not have to tolerate abuse, of any kind, from anyone, including their parents. No child should feel a duty of care or loyalty towards those who harm them, yet that's a pattern so easily learned in parent-child relationships. The lines between love and abuse get blurred. When I've apologised to Emilia in the past, and she replied, 'That's okay,' I made sure to tell her that, 'No, it's *not* okay.' Children need to know that they are deserving of love, respect and kindness.

We all royally screw up from time-to-time and apologising is non-negotiable. You mess up, you apologise. Don't listen to social dogma that tells you not to show weakness to your child, not to let them have the upper hand, not to cry in front of them. Apologise. Make amends. Show that you are human. Model healthy conflict resolution. Demonstrate that adults are not always in the right, that adults get it wrong - *very* wrong - at times. Allow them to challenge your behaviour and call you out. Admitting your mistake is a strength, not a weakness. Every screw up is an opportunity to learn and commit to doing better. But repeating the same mistake and apologising for the same mistake over and over again doesn't cut it either - we don't want this pattern to become 'safe' and familiar!

When an ex-partner first hit me, I accepted his apology. Then it happened again. And again. I stayed with him for nearly three years. The physical abuse - which 'only' happened on four occasions - was nothing compared to the emotional abuse that stripped my confidence, self-esteem, and spirit. It took a moment of insanity (or perhaps divine intervention?!) and me wrapping my hands tightly around his throat to realise how toxic our relationship was. Only then did I leave – to keep *him* safe, not me!

We are taught what to tolerate. We are taught that we are responsible for other people's happiness – and rage. We are taught to be both complicit and submissive of abusive behaviour, not to make a fuss or speak up. We are taught to please and appease at the expense of our own comfort and safety. We are taught to be the 'victim' (note that I'm talking about dynamics, not actual victimisation). And when our pain becomes unbearable, and we can no longer contain it, we turn into the 'perpetrator', physically or verbally unleashing it onto the weakest and most vulnerable: children.

When we fall into a pattern of yelling at our kids, emotionally detaching, withholding love and presence as punishment, spanking them, or using shame or other oppressive means to control their behaviour, we are teaching them that abusive behaviour is okay. We are teaching them the kinds of behaviours to tolerate in future relationships. We are teaching them the types of relationships to expect and deserve. We are teaching them how to treat others. We are normalising these dynamics, so that they feel safe and familiar when repeated later on in life. And - unconsciously - we are teaching them that they are unworthy, undeserving, and unlovable. Eventually, they stop loving themselves.

A child who stops loving themselves becomes an adult who doesn't love themselves, and who seeks unhealthy and destructive ways to self-soothe and fill the emptiness inside.

Abusive relationships. Alcohol dependency. Bulimia. Depression. Attempted suicide. Promiscuity. Toxic friendships. Anxiety. Self-neglect. And a pattern of self-sabotage every time life is good because of a deeply entrenched belief that I'm not worthy or deserving of love, only punishment. This is a summary of my story, the patterns of which still play out today, especially in those moments of unconscious parenting.

Breaking the Cycle

We'd be naive to think that we can raise children free from pain. Pain and suffering are an inevitable part of the human condition. We can't always protect our children. We have no control over their experiences and the hurt that others may cause. But we can protect them from ourselves, which - uncomfortable as it is - is where their pain begins. There are no guarantees that our actions won't cause our children harm, no matter how conscious we are, but we can minimise the damage. We need to look inside ourselves and face our deepest, darkest, innermost wounds, and be radically honest about the part we've played in enabling what is, for the most part, a deeply abusive culture.

We need to be honest about the ways we neglect and abuse ourselves and the dependency we place on others - our partners, friends, and children - to fill the void. As much as we want to love our children unconditionally, few of us do. Our children are burdened by sets of rules and conditions to make them more acceptable and lovable, rules that we ourselves learnt and have carried down the lineage. No one taught us to love ourselves; we can't learn self-love from those who didn't love themselves, either. But now we have the awareness, we can learn, and we can sow the seeds of self-love in our kids. The more we can instil a strong sense of self-love and worthiness in our children and model interdependence instead of co-dependency, the less likely they'll be to rely on others to give it to them. This doesn't

mean that children raised in the happiest and healthiest of environments are immune from abusive or destructive experiences; the dynamics are so insidious it can happen to anyone. But we need to be aware of the role that we, as parents, play. It starts with us. If we want to break the cycle and free our children from *our* pain, we need to do the work.

Stepping into a new parenting paradigm means unshackling ourselves from generations of pain, trauma, and programming. It means removing the childist lens through which we have been indoctrinated to view children, and treating them with the respect, kindness, and compassion that they deserve. Children don't have to earn their place in this world, they already belong. They don't owe us anything and shouldn't be punished for being born; for most of us, that was our choice. As is how we choose to treat them, moment to moment, even when it feels like we're losing control.

It starts with making a commitment to being the change and the person we needed as a child. It doesn't mean being the perfect parent or raising perfect kids. It doesn't mean you'll never screw up. But it does mean that when you do, you have the awareness to self-reflect, own your part, show yourself kindness and compassion, and move forward with grace.

Being a more 'conscious' parent is a daily practise, and not always an easy one because we all have our unconscious moments. It comes down to choice, and re-committing daily to those choices (especially on those difficult days – every day is a chance to start anew). I can choose to raise my kids to live as the authentic expression of themselves, even the parts that challenge societal norms (and my own conditioning). I can choose not to centre my own experience when they have an emotional meltdown, and hold space regardless of who's watching or how I'm feeling. I can choose to recognise my triggers and prioritise my self-care so that they don't bubble over into my parenting. And I can choose to advocate for my kids, so they know that at least one person in their life has their back, no matter what.

If this chapter has resonated with you and you want to move away from abusive dynamics within your parenting, here are a few pointers to get you started:

1) Reflect on the kind of parent you desire to be versus the parent you currently are. This isn't about dropping into shame or guilt, rather bringing awareness to your style of parenting and whether or not it is truly aligned to you, your heart, and your values. Tune into the parts of you that feel

conflicted, and where in your body the sensation of discomfort arises. For me, any time I behave in a way that causes internal struggle and contradicts my moral compass, I feel a pang in my heart. Be radically honest about the behaviours (yours) that you want to change. When we can sit with the discomfort of our own vulnerability and fallibility, we can then begin to move forwards with awareness and grace, and commit to those changes. This is an entirely new way of being, so it will take time. Being more 'conscious' is a daily practise, and recommitting daily to the changes that you want to make. Be kind and patient with yourself. And know that, on those inevitable bad days, every moment is a fresh start and opportunity to start anew.

2) Begin to recognise the ego-state that you are in during those highly-charged moments with your children. This will take a lot of practise, but once you start to notice the driving force behind your own behaviour, it's easier to come back to yourself and reconnect, firstly with you, then with your child(ren).

If you are in a **child ego-state**, you are replaying

behaviours, thoughts, and feelings from your childhood, so possibly 'throwing your toys out the pram', flipping your lid in a seemingly irrational way, or being hurtful with your words. If you are in a **parent ego-state**, you are expressing thoughts, feelings, and behaviours copied from a parent or parental figure. This is when we cringe when we hear a parent's voice coming out of our mouth! Quite often, there are certain traits and behaviours that we don't wish to emulate from our parents because of our childhood experiences ... though when we drop into the parent ego-state, we mimic them anyway! If, however, you are in an **adult ego-state**, your thoughts, feelings, and behaviours are direct responses to the here and now. In this state, you're more likely to remain calm and less reactive. In an ideal world, this is the place we'd like to be with our children, however, unprocessed trauma means we typically flit between that of the child or parent.

3) If you have grown up in a volatile environment or experienced any form of abusive relationship, particularly when you were younger, you may have found it difficult to manage your own anger or 'explosive moments' since having children - parenting can be very re-traumatizing!

Know that you are not alone and that support is available for you should you need it. If you are in the UK, ask your GP for a referral to a therapist, or find a healing modality that resonates with you. Do not be afraid to ask for help (though please seek a trauma-informed therapist, where possible). EFT (Energy Freedom Technique) really helped me to start releasing some of the layers of my own trauma which, energetically, had a noticeable impact on my children. Don't get me wrong, there's still a long way to go - these wounds cut deep! But it's a step in a more positive, peaceful direction.

Let's Reflect

Take ownership of your guilt, and use it to effect positive change. When you know better, you do better.

We all make mistakes. We all screw up, no matter how 'healed' or 'conscious' we are. Apologise. Make amends. Admitting your mistakes is a strength, not a weakness. It's healthy for children to learn that parents are human and can get things *very* wrong at times, instead of teaching them that adults (authority figures) are always right!

Make a commitment to being the change and the person you needed as a child. It doesn't mean being the perfect parent or raising perfect kids. You'll still make mistakes, and that's OK. Own your part, show yourself kindness and compassion, and move forward with grace.

Every moment is the opportunity for a fresh start!

And lastly … it's *never* too late!

The original version of this chapter was first featured in **The Silent Scream** *by Maria Alfieri, available from all major online retailers.*

About the Author

Michelle Catanach is a writer, illustrator, and speaker of uncomfortable truths! She believes that authentic self-expression is a birth right and that we owe it to ourselves and our children to live a life of integrity and alignment to who we truly are, no matter how much the world tries to cage us. Michelle believes in the transformational, healing, and revolutionary power of the written word. She runs writing retreats and workshops, is a non-fiction ghost writer for entrepreneurs, and helps indie authors to write and self-publish their books. She also indulges her fascination for psychology by studying for a degree in social psychology.

Connect with Michelle:

Website: michelle@michellecatanach.co.uk

Instagram: www.instagram.com/michelle_catanach

Her latest book *Uncaged*, a collection of raw and honest poetry which explores the themes of sexuality, motherhood, and mental health, among other topics, is available from Amazon.

Look out for Michelle's upcoming *Being Human* podcast, book club, and writing groups.

The Perfect Parent Trap

By Maria Alfieri

'When it comes to accepting ourselves as imperfect, we set the tone for our children. The degree to which they accept their imperfections tends to be the degree to which we accept and honour our own.'

~ Dr Shefali Tsabary

Perfectionism is often thought of as a positive trait, however, it doesn't allow for shades of grey or anything 'in-between'. It holds us in a fixed mind-set; we pass or we fail. We are good or bad. We are worthy or unworthy. Perfectionism is paradoxically a self-defeating way to live; mistakes are a necessary part of learning. By avoiding mistakes at any cost, a perfectionist can make it harder to reach their own high expectations and goals. Perfectionism, therefore, is ultimately not about achievement and growth, but rather a shield against the pain of blame, judgement, or shame, as researched by Professor Brené Brown.

When we feel shame about ourselves, perfectionism becomes the buffer zone between ourselves and the rest of the world – the armour we wear to navigate our way through the battlefield of life. Living entrenched in such deep shame means we never really accept ourselves and are, in fact, always running from the truth of who we are. We live in a negative space, our lives constantly riddled with regret, judgement, self-doubt, and a sense of never-ending impeding failure. When it comes to parenting, perfectionism becomes the dictator of the household, spreading fear and shame to maintain control through its inflexible rules and high expectations. Perfectionism advocates staying inside the lines and avoiding the mess that we, as humans, are inevitably going to encounter; any parent will tell you how impossible this is to maintain where children are concerned!

Becoming a parent has been the biggest challenge for my inner perfectionist. I spent most of my youth fearing being 'wrong' and prided myself on being an 'A' grade student because I believed that one little letter gave my life value and meaning. Motherhood has helped change my perspective and encouraged me to not always play it safe within the boundaries of black and white thinking, and to embrace the vibrancy and colour of life instead. My parenting journey has shown me how perfectionism only serves as a rope around my neck, which chokes me out of so many learning opportunities and experiences. This also applies to the learning opportunities that arise from parenting failures - those moments that teach us to do better next time.

I don't think I've ever (knowingly) pushed the perfection agenda onto my children, and I've certainly never directly told them that they should strive for perfection or that they need to be the best; 'try your best' has always been my mantra to them. Yet, trying my best as their mother hasn't always felt good enough, as I've felt pressured both internally and externally to meet an ideal of motherhood that just doesn't exist.

I would never advocate to my children adhering to, or being subservient to, in the same way I always have. I've often feared being true to myself, which is something I battle on a daily basis, flitting between the poles of rigidity and fluidity; rigidity being the constraints of perfectionism and fluidity being the result of being true to myself. I want my children to have a growth mind-set; to know that mistakes - or 'the mess' as my inner perfectionist would call it - are where we learn, grow, and change. I want my children to be inquisitive about their imperfections, for them to use them as opportunities to self-reflect and move forward, not to use them as a stick to beat themselves with. A growth mind-set I have learnt is essential to being able to manage the ebb and flow of life, rather than trying to resist it through perfectionist tendencies. But I've also learnt that children do as we do and not as we say, and trying to teach imperfection as someone whose foundations are built on perfectionism has caused much inner turmoil for me.

I've had to surrender the idea that I can mould and shape my children into being reflections of my perfect parenting (which, of course, is not perfect), and acknowledge that, in order to be the best parent that I can, I need to let go of any pre-conceived ideas I had about who and what I thought my children 'should' be, and let them discover for themselves who they are.

Letting go of any expectations I might have initially had about who my children would become has been a lot less challenging than letting go of my expectations of myself as a parent. My inner perfectionist wants me to be a perfect parent. It wants me to be the fully conscious parent at all times, without any of those unconscious parenting moments where we find ourselves triggered, angered, and stressed. It wants me to be fully present at all times, to all four of my children, giving my all at any given moment. Anything less isn't good enough. I worry that, as a result of my imperfect parenting, my children will be damaged and continually ruminate over my parenting mistakes. My inner critic is fuelled as I scroll through social media. It's so hard to compare and keep up with everyone else: the online bake-off's between parents; the over-the-top birthday celebrations for children who can barely even walk; the families training together to run bi-monthly marathons.

And then there is the parenting competition at school – whose children have the best World Book Day costumes? Whose Easter bonnet is the most fabulous? Whose children raised the most money at the school fun run? We lose sight of the learning intention for the child behind such events, of the opportunity for them to be creative and innovative, parents hijacking the process to demonstrate their wonderful parenting skills rather than children being given the opportunity to display their own achievements.

Alongside the internet wars, the judgemental looks, and the one upping from parents in the playground, there is also the increasing pressure on parents to be 'woke', to be in the constant process of healing their own wounds, and to be breaking free from family cycles and inherited generational trauma. I'm not suggesting that we shouldn't be working towards these goals, but when we inevitably slip up, perfectionism will have us catastrophising. Even without perfectionist tendencies, is it any wonder that parenting these days can feel so completely overwhelming? We aren't just trying to parent our children but we are also trying to parent ourselves along the way, shedding skins, patterns, and behaviours that no longer serve us, and that we know certainly do not serve our children. When we are conscious of our triggers and our non-serving behaviours, and yet still choose fear over love in moments of reactivity, it is easy to feel ashamed of ourselves as parents.

But when it comes to parenting, shaming ourselves in this way is corrosive. The fear of not being the perfect parent, the guilt – it erodes positivity, happiness and freedom. It inhibits our creativity and our innovation and, in turn, impedes on all of these things for our children. If our children see us owning our mistakes and bad decisions, and watch as we try and figure out what went wrong and how we can do better next time, they will be better equipped to problem solve themselves. When they see us comparing ourselves to others, they will do the same. We need to teach them that life is not a competition but about growth of character. When we constantly have our eyes on others, we are never looking at ourselves – knowledge of the self really is the key to a happier, freer life.

As parents, just as with anything in life, we need to lead by example. When our children see that we are unable to accept our imperfections, how will they ever accept theirs? When my expectations of myself are so high, I know I inadvertently undermine my efforts to teach my children about the gift of imperfection. It doesn't matter how much I tell them to use mistakes as learning opportunities if they repeatedly see me punishing myself for my own.

There is a difference between being conscientious and being a perfectionist. And for me, it's about striking a balance. Perfectionism isn't about setting goals or working hard – it's about the critical inner voice that tells us that we are not good enough. For perfectionists, their performance is inextricable from who they are. When they don't succeed they feel more than disappointment – they feel shame, and shame is a soul-eating emotion. Shame is something I never want my children to feel about themselves, and yet that is exactly the message I send to them when I feel shame about my own failures.

I lived so much of my life looking to others and external sources to guide me – give me instruction and I can follow, leave me with a blank canvas and I'm terrified by the endless possibilities, by the thought of 'getting it wrong'. I've learnt not to be so terrified, that I do not fall neatly into a pre-defined category, and to trust my instincts, to let my spirit and soul guide me. Living life by other people's expectations or limitations (or even our own perceived expectations and limitations) prohibits growth of character. Growth, I've learnt, is an essential part of maintaining good mental health. I want my children to embrace the blank canvas of their lives, to listen to the voice inside - not the inner bully regurgitating external ideals, but the true voice speaking from the very depths of their soul. And this is something they'll learn to do through quiet time, mindfulness, and meditation, which is exactly how we, as adults, can reconnect with this innate part of ourselves.

I used to think that rest time was dead time - if I wasn't learning, achieving, or doing, I was wasting my time. It doesn't help that these are views often perpetuated by society and culture. I've had to learn that sometimes the most productive thing I can do is to take some time out, and to allow myself some rest and recuperation, time to download my thoughts, and shut out the 'should be doing' - not something that is encouraged in this 24-hour world in which we live.

The first step in the battle against perfectionism and that inner critic is self-compassion. When I realised I didn't want my kids to ever feel about themselves the way that I did, I knew I had to work on changing how I felt about myself. If I want my kids to know their own worth then first I had better work on knowing mine.

Acknowledging that you are a perfectionist parent is certainly one of the first steps you can take to not only improve your parenting skills, but almost every area of your life. Letting go of perfectionism isn't easy, but when you're able to be more gentle and compassionate with yourself, you'll naturally find yourself being more gentle and compassionate with others. Being a perfectionist stresses you out to the max and, in turn, puts stress on your children. You and your children will find yourself living in a calmer environment once you begin to reign in that inner perfectionist when it starts to get out of control.

Other tips to help both you and your children in the battle against perfectionism are:

- Focus on the things you do get right and give yourself credit when things go well. It's easy to dismiss the positives, but celebrating your wins is an important part of overcoming shame-based thinking.

- Send healthy messages about failure. Remember, a fixed mind-set (perfectionism) will keep you stuck in rigid cycles and unhelpful thinking. A growth mind-set is where you can embrace your failures which will help you to grow and change.

- Pay attention to your (and your child's) effort, and not the outcome. It's about trying and moving forward, not being successful or unsuccessful. This just sends unhealthy messages about worth.

- Challenge your thinking and learn to separate yourself from your thoughts. Ask yourself if your thoughts are really true. Is there any evidence to support them? Are these thoughts helping me or hurting me? Ask yourself what will happen if you let go of these thoughts. Learning mindfulness and meditation can be really useful for this.

- Don't compare yourself to others, and don't doubt your parenting choices; you make decisions based on your own unique family situation and both yours and your children's needs. These will not be the same as anybody else's.

- Talk to other parents willing to make themselves vulnerable and be truthful about their own parenting experiences. Surrounding yourself with a good support network and removing yourself from those clinging onto toxic social scripting and judgement will be really beneficial to you on your parenting journey.

And remember, if you are used to being a high achiever, it can be extremely difficult to pull back when it comes to your children. But kids who think they have to be perfect (whether you send this as a direct or inadvertent message) are at a higher risk themselves of developing perfectionism and many of the associated mental health problems. The mantra I now live by is *Be Kind*. Firstly to yourself. And then it becomes a lot easier to be kind, compassionate, understanding, and non-judgemental to your children who, in turn, can be those things towards themselves and others.

Let's Reflect

Mistakes are where we learn, grow and change.

Time to drop the guilt! It erodes positivity, happiness and freedom, inhibiting our creativity and innovation and, in turn, impeding on all of these things for our children.

Living by other people's expectations (including your own) prohibits growth of character. Growth is an essential part of maintaining good mental health.

Learn to listen to the voice inside through quiet time, mindfulness, and meditation.

Show self-compassion to drown out the inner critic. In time, you will start to feel differently about yourself.

About the Author

Maria is a mother of four children who frequently challenge her inner perfectionist and have been her greatest life teachers. Pre-motherhood Maria worked as an English teacher in secondary schools, and has spent the last two years advocating for better mental and emotional health across society. Her anthology *The Silent Scream* highlights the power of connection in the process of healing, growth and change for better mental and emotional wellbeing. Profits from the anthology are going to Heads On, a mental health and safeguarding charity for the NHS.

Connect with Maria:

Website: www.mariaalfieri.com
Twitter: www.twitter.com/mariaalfieri6
Instagram: www.instagram.com/mariaualfieri

The Silent Scream: An Anthology of Despair, Struggle and Hope is available in hardback, paperback, and on Kindle from Amazon, Nook, Barnes & Noble, and Waterstones online.

Self- Compassion in the Heart of Parenting

By Maria Kefalogianni

'The only constant in life is change.'

~ Heraclitus

I invite you to pause and ponder this for a minute …

Despite Heraclitus's quote being true for us all, it strikes me as a uniquely (and perhaps necessary) paradox that we, as society, are incessantly searching for answers. We look for ultimatums, solutions, quick fixes for everything. There are many parenting books out there offering tips and direct advice on 'how to be a good parent' or 'what to do when …'. They have their place, of course. However, I often wonder to what extent they contribute towards an 'external locus of evaluation' (Rogers, 1961). Having an 'external locus of evaluation' vs an 'internal locus of evaluation' means that, the more we expect to find the answers from a source located 'outside' of us, the further away we move from our own inner wisdom and inner authentic knowing.

Theories around parenting continuously change. The paradigm feels to have shifted towards understanding the child as a person with their own rights. There is greater emphasis on the protection of the rights of the child. This leaves me wondering if, in this process, we have somehow become too child-centred and neglected the parent. Stress in parenthood has become so common, like beans on toast. Have we forgotten what we already know? Have we detached so far away from our true selves that parenting feels hard nowadays? Furthermore, I have observed that there is little written work on the 'parent's journey', describing it as it *is* - unscripted and in all its rawness and honesty, just like our days as parents. It's as if we are all collectively trying to learn how to be a parent but are hesitant to share our daily stories. Our voices.

Beneath our search for answers, I hear a longing for validation, reassurance, affirmation of our parenting capacity and worth, and so on. A collective longing for us, as parents, to be re-homed back to ourselves.

This chapter aims to bring the parent into the heart of parenting. I am passionate about illuminating my own experiences and sharing my raw, honest, authentic voice - just as I experience some of these moments in my parenting journey. Moments that scar us all inside, moments echoed from our past. I wish to share my voice in service to those parents who wish to catch a breath, in recognition of the struggles but also the rewards. My aim is not to teach you what I believe you already know ... although perhaps you don't know that you know. I aim to point you to the wisdom and knowledge that already lies within you.

The Perfect Start

The moment of soul-conception of my first child, Iosef, is where my reflections begin. It is summer of 2014. I find myself lying silently on a Cretan beach under the majestic full moon and starry sky. I remain silent for a while when I suddenly begin sobbing. It feels like a moment of melting, of great undoing. Minutes later, I manage to find my voice and tell my husband: 'I have no idea what just happened, it felt compelling. The only way I can describe it is as if Mother Earth was speaking to me *through* me.' A year in, I found this memory and these words recorded in my notes on my phone. Iosef's (soul) conception happened either that night or a few days before. I feel he gave that night to us like a precious gift … leading to a perfect home - birth. A majestic journey into the abyss of love began. Those first days, first weeks, first year, I felt the depths of a love, as deep as the ocean, as vast as the skies. Love that I never thought I was capable of embodying.

Welcome to parenthood!

Speaking the Unspoken in our Collective Parent Psyche

I often say that parenthood is like an all-inclusive five star hotel, with *all* its highs and lows. Soon, the sparkle of parenthood began to fade - a gradual undoing of perfectionism ensued. Shortly after birth, the sleepless nights started, the irritability, the angst, the pains, the dread of death. A counter reflex response to the depth of love that I felt. The transitions … the end of breastfeeding transitioning to solid food. I felt the loss so deeply in my body in each one of these phases. In every significant threshold moment, a mother milestone was also achieved. A deeper letting go and trust to the river of life and all its cycles. I recall crying the first time that I had to replace his clothes with a bigger size! My baby was growing so fast. I felt a loss; it felt like he was slipping through my fingertips, like water. At the time, I questioned the tears. Soon, I realised it was a moment of embodied inner wisdom that love and death in parenthood go together. A manifestation of the pendulum that explains the dance between the need to control and a compelling pull towards freedom.

Every transition signifies a new era that I was called to be present for. I felt the weight of responsibility in responding to his moment to moment changes. I felt I was called to be a chameleon on a desert island – 'the parent-land' known only by me. At times, it felt scary, lonely, isolating.

There are times that it can all get too much. I lose my temper. I shout. A lot. Then, I instantly retreat into the corrosive guilt land. This guilt has its grip tightly around my heart. It squeezes her so hard that I have to gasp for air sometimes. In those moments, I can hear my mind's games replaying a familiar script: 'I am not a good enough mother.' Sometimes, this inner tension and conflict cannot be contained, and I find myself snapping out in a fascinating high pitch I never thought I was capable of. This guilt has been a common visitor in my heart. What am I supposed to do with it? Indulging its power breeds more. I cannot deny it either.

The very successful protective mechanism (denial) has long left me since my psychotherapy training. Sometimes, I pray for it to return. It is in those moments that I clearly notice how my long rehearsed and ingenious strategies of dissociation play out. Distraction at its best and denying the consequences of my actions. Running away from taking radical responsibility in the moment. This shield is well worn and hard wired. Any smell of blame from the outside and it explodes into anger or manifests in a need to hide away – like a little girl frightened of being blamed and judged. A girl who built a wall around her in order to be protected. This has been my most familiar comfort zone for a *long* time (Redford, 2015).

Despite parenthood being an 'all-inclusive' business, we keep finding more comfort in splitting and categorising our feelings into good and bad. Useful and not useful. Feelings of 'should' as a parent and feelings of 'should not'. Despite being an all-inclusive hotel, we keep going for the take-aways!

Is what I describe familiar to you? Have you ever felt like this? Know that you are not alone. Behind your well-built walls, I wish to come close, sing to you, and remind you how loved you are. I wish to whisper in your ear: 'I can see how much you struggle at the moment. I've been there too. I wish I was there when you first felt compelled as a child to hide your feelings out of fear. I wish I was there to hold you, to tell you how safe you are, and to remind you it is *not* your responsibility to protect anyone from your feelings. Let me carry this burden for you and let your tears flow. I am here.'

What parents need most in those moments is self-compassion. A companion during these wild waves of emotion. Surf with me on the waves of our humanness with the compassion you deserve. In those moments, I do not want to be told what I did wrong. I know. My soul knows and aches. Being a psychotherapist has its own disadvantages. There are times that my mind races at the speed of light calculating the level of 'trauma' I am imprinting on my child during a 'difficult moment'. I do not want to dress up these moments as just 'moments'. At the time, they feel like an eternity. Time freezes – so is my heart. They feel like they last forever … and they hold hostage my heart which has locked into fear, and lost touch with the abyss of love lying underneath.

Guilt is like our invisible child. We hold onto it for dear life. We nourish it and keep feeding it with a ton of self-attacks and self-berating statements. We grow it through incessant invisible comparisons in our heads. It is like a phantom whisper behind each one of our actions, saying, 'Is this ok?' 'Was this right?' 'Maybe I shouldn't have done this.' Behind this, there seems to be a lurking belief that there are 'answers' or, even worse, 'right' answers for parenthood.

My suspicion is that this might also apply to you. Is your mind at times caught up in a spiral dance of negative self-talk statements? Feeling guilty and, consequently, feeling critical for feeling guilty, and so on.

What if your guilt has a crucial purpose? What is driving your guilt, if not an abundant ocean of love towards your children? This ocean appears to get blocked because our hearts, in the moment, struggle to hold enough compassion for ourselves. How then will we be able to be with our children?

Self-Compassion

Take a moment to ask yourself: how were you cared for, and how was conflict resolved in your childhood? What do you really want from yourself as a parent? What is it you really wish for yourself during the difficult parenting moments? I would not be surprised if some of the answers you give are along the lines of 'to not feel like this' OR 'to not yell or scream' OR 'to not feel guilty'. Saying no to those moments is like denying yourself to yourself. Self-compassion is non-selective but all-inclusive. According to research, there are numerous blocks and myths around self-compassion. It is often seen as self-indulgence. I see this often in my practice as a therapist, especially in mothers. We are conditioned to believe that loving ourselves is selfish! Isn't it more self-indulgent to bask in a sea of self-criticism, entertaining and perpetuating an unconscious belief around our omnipotence and infallibility?

Self-compassion is qualitatively different to self-kindness or self-care. It links with a deep recognition that we are all humans. Perfectly imperfect. It requires an element of mindful presence vs. over identification during the difficult moments. In order to tap into this inner space, we are called to mindfully notice and accept what is presenting itself within us, and not avoid it. A full acknowledgement of *all* that is there. To be able to do this, we need to feel that our self-love and energy bucket is at least half-full so that we have the energy to deal with the emotions this acknowledgement often unleashes.

Gentle Note: This can feel hard! Self-compassion requires very gentle steps, and perhaps good therapy! It is super important for me to note that research has found that feelings of warmth or gentle reassurance back to oneself can often feel threatening and frightening for high self-critics. So, it is very understandable why people struggle to access their soothing systems (Gilbert, 2000). I see it in my therapy practice day in, day out. It requires a patient, gentle companion to help you feel safe enough so that you can drop the very valuable defences and walls you built to protect yourself throughout the years. If you struggle to offer yourself compassion, know that you are not failing. The part of you that is struggling needs your compassion to start with.

Quite often, the conflicts with ourselves or our kids do not even belong in the present, but the past. Mark Wolynn (*It Didn't Start With You*, 2015) stipulates that we all carry inherited family trauma. This is inevitable. Our purpose is to create a home for it so that it can all be felt, recognised, acknowledged, and not exiled … so that it can be healed.

My story is not new. Your story is not new. What is unfolding in these moments is a mirror to aspects of old generational trauma that has not been fully integrated in the family of lineage, and therefore not fully integrated in the human body that you inhabit. Our children become our mirrors. Siegel and Hartzell, (2003), pg.28, write, 'When unresolved issues are writing our [parents'] life story, we are not our own auto biographers; we are merely recorders of how the past continues, often without our awareness, to intrude upon our present experience and shape our future directions.' This means that we tend to react versus respond. We are caught up by primary emotional states and stepping away, in the moment, from our neocortex brain – which is capable of rational, mindful decision making. We lose each other when what we crave the most is to connect with each other.

Once we manage some level of self-compassion through a gentle responsiveness to the needs of ourselves, a space opens within us that is more capable of attuning to the needs of our children. In this way, we see that self-compassion is actually relational! If we are regulated in the moment, we can then help our children to create an 'internal working model' - an internalised map of how they see the world and how safe they feel in it (Bowlby, 1969) - by helping them create cellular memories of being soothed and regulated. When they grow to become adults, they will be more likely to have cultivated a compassionate way to self-to-self relating (Gilbert & Procter, 2006). In a nutshell, investing in yourself is, in fact, investing in your children.

Similarly, Carl Rogers talked about the innate tendency in each human being towards self-actualisation and growth. Every human being and parent has this in themselves. He also talked about a crucial principle in establishing therapeutic connection with clients – 'the therapist needs to be in psychological contact' 'a state of inner congruence' with themselves. A state of inner congruence is a state of awareness of what is going on within, married with an attitude of acceptance and compassion (Rogers, 1961). This seems to suggest, like above, that in order to be in good contact and have a connection with others, we first and primarily need to establish what is happening within ourselves.

Insights / Learnings / Pointers

In time, I have appreciated more that my difficult days are not written in stone. I/you have the most amazing and powerful tool in your hands. Mindful awareness of your inner states. Language to put this into words. Language to help you concretise the pain that has been residue in your/our hearts and DNA for generations. It is crucial to find the language and the courage to vocalise our inner feelings in order to integrate these experiences in an embodied manner. I have learned that holding the little girl in me is a crucial step towards maturity as an adult. I have learnt that expecting, with entitlement, this level of compassion from the outside often leaves me in deep despair and disappointment. How on earth can the other person offer this to us when we are struggling to offer it to ourselves? This business called parenthood is calling forth my soul to speak the language that my mind never learnt ... but is one that we all know and hold deep inside.

I also appreciate and fully accept that, regardless of the level of awareness I hold, it is the job of my 'monkey mind' to keep its familiar narrative. The familiar scripts might never go away. However, in my experience, they become quieter. Slowly, and with ongoing exploration and inner healing, a new voice emerges to counter balance the old and familiar one. In fact, I now feel that my mind is my ally as it helps to bring about all that is to be healed. If you are daring, you don't even need to believe your thoughts, as Jack Kornfield says. Though this is a simple sentence, I recognise it takes a lot of patience, self-acceptance and practicing mindfulness.

During those agonising parenting moments, your whole brain is in an actual battle, according to Siegel & Bryson (2012). Your left-brain grasps for order and control. It is logical and linear. Your right-brain is holistic, nonverbal, communicating at all times in ways other than words. Personally, in those moments, my main default saviour is my breath. Cultivating mindful breathing creates a wonderful space between myself and my emotions. It is a conscious breath; it is *free* and accessible as my most powerful tool, always. In that inhale, I am reminded that there is tomorrow … this is a fleeting passing moment in the face of eternity and nothing else … this too shall pass. Through this space I offer to myself, I open a door, a portal, to my child's heart. I then feel more able to see things through his eyes. This helps to ground me and bring me back into the present moment. I recall regulating my own body through breath as my way of settling my son to bed as a baby. The results were magnificent! I still default to my breath during the tremendous power of the tantrums.

Below, I provide some pointers for further reflection. Take some time to either journal or reflect on them, through sitting in silence or with a trusted friend.

What would it take for you to hold the shame, the sense of exposure and the fear that you experience in deep compassion? What would this even look like? If you struggle to find an answer, bring to mind a compassionate friend or ally. What would they tell you in the moments you struggle the most?

What would it take if you allowed yourself three minutes or three pauses during your day to ask yourself, 'How are you doing today?' and make space for your genuine answer to emerge?

Can those house chores wait a little longer? How would it feel if you allowed yourself two minutes of conscious breathing while lying on the bed doing nothing, listening to music? Can you allow yourself to do whatever makes your heart sing for a moment?

Have you got enough of a support network around you to share your ups and downs? Talking uninhibited about all the ugly dark moments of parenthood can feel so liberating.

Whatever you choose to do to ease those difficult parenting moments, it has to feel congruent with who you are.

Lastly, if I was to give you some direct advice, it would be this: do the best you can, as I trust you already do. Open a bank account, and start saving money for their therapy – the best advice given to me that I cherish to this day.

Go easy, go gently ... you deserve it.

Let's Reflect

Self-compassion recognises that we are all human – perfectly imperfect.

The conflict with ourselves or our kids do not even belong in the present, but the past. Our purpose is to create a home for it so that it can all be felt, recognised, acknowledged, and healed.

Once we manage some level of self-compassion, a space opens within us that is more capable of attuning to the needs of our children.

Guilt means that our hearts, in the moment, struggle to hold enough compassion for ourselves, making it more difficult to be with our children.

About the Author

Maria Kefalogianni is a lecturer in Counselling & Psychotherapy at the University of Salford, UK. She is a module leader and tutor on mindfulness based modules, leads on Bereavement & Loss module, and co-leads the Post-Graduate Certificate in Supervision in the Helping Relationships. Besides this, she holds a private psychotherapy practice for young people and adults, as well as offering supervision/consultation to professionals. Her practice is person-centred and compassion focused with a keen interest in mindfulness and the transpersonal. Her research is around somatic/embodied ways of knowing, and the role of arts in therapy and life. She is also currently in training to become a sound healing practitioner. Her self-care is through nature, yoga, dance, and her ongoing spiritual practise.

Connect with Maria:

Facebook: www.facebook.com/Counselling4You

Twitter: @MariaKef14

LinkedIn: www.linkedin.com/in/maria-kefalogianni-32169314

REFERENCES:

- Bowlby, J. (1969). Attachment: Attachment and loss, Vol. 1. London: Hogarth.
- Gilbert, P. (2000). Social mentalities: Internal 'social' conflicts and the role of inner warmth and compassion in cognitive therapy. In P. Gilbert, & K.G. Bailey (Eds), Genes on the couch: Explorations in evolutionary psychotherapy (pp. 118-150). Hove: Brunner-Routledge
- Gilbert, P., & Procter, S. (2006). Compassionate mind training for people with high shame and self-criticism: A pilot study of a group therapy approach. Clinical Psychology and Psychotherapy, 13, 353-379
- Redford, A. (2015). The boy who built a wall around himself . Illustrated by Kara Simpson. Jessica Kingsley Publishers
- Rogers, C. (1961). On becoming a person. A therapist's view of Psychotherapy. Houghton Mifflin, 1961;

- Siegel, D, J., & Hartzel, M. (2014). *Parenting from the Inside out. How a deeper self-understanding can help you raise children who thrive. 10th ed.* The Penguin Group.
- Siegel, D.J., & Bryson, T. (2012) . *The Whole-Brain Child: 12 Proven Strategies to Nurture Your Child's Mind*
- Wolynn, M. (2016) . *It didn't start with you. How inherited trauma shapes who we are and how to end the cycle* .

Nurturing the True Essence of Your Child

By Clare Ford

'The day came when the risk to remain tight in a bud was more painful than the risk it took to blossom.'

~ Anais Nin

We are born to live as the fullest expression of our whole selves - physically, spiritually, and emotionally - yet through life events, trauma, and conditioning, we typically disconnect from the essence of who we are. Much dis-ease can be attributed to abandoning and forgetting our true self as we seek external means to fill the void. However, who we are never leaves us but is lying dormant, waiting to be reawakened. Our children are our best teachers, reflecting, mirroring, and pointing us back into the direction of our soul, where we can reconnect with those lost parts of our own inner child and become whole once again.

For the most part, I had a happy childhood and felt loved by my grandmother, who cared for me while my mum and dad worked managing pubs and hotels. My mother was very busy and I don't really remember being held or kissed by her. She used to fall asleep reading me stories at bedtime and often rushed us around from pillar to post.

I clearly remember a balmy spring afternoon, when I was sitting in the pub garden, gazing with wonder at the butterflies and bees, busily flitting from flower to flower, and enjoying the tickle of the ladybird on my finger. I was aware of colours shimmering around me and felt that I could hear all the little sounds that nature was making. I felt very at home, comfortable with the richness of the lush grass and the warm earth surrounding me. So when I was called inside, I didn't want to go.

My mother got angry. She was in a hurry and needed me inside, but I was daydreaming, making up stories about flower fairies in my head. I was always reprimanded for daydreaming; for having my head in the clouds (I loved cloud gazing and star gazing and still do!), and was being asked to 'hurry up' and 'get a move on' and 'stop being so silly'. There wasn't time to listen to my ramblings or to look at the world through my eyes.

As a child, I had 'pretend' friends and was always making up games in my head and I enjoyed playing on my own. I also sensed things before they happened. I could see auras - although I didn't know that was what they were called - but the more I spoke about these things to the adults around me, the more I was told that I was 'making things up' and 'of course there's nothing there', or that I had an over-active imagination. Slowly, I began to realise that what I saw, felt, and sensed wasn't important, and that it was safer for that part of me to disappear altogether and become invisible.

And that was when the disconnection began. The disconnection of my spiritual self and the need to 'people please'. To show up in a way that was 'acceptable' and 'understood'. To show up in a way that was measurable by 'normal' standards. I became a tomboy – honing my more masculine energies of competitiveness, not being too needy or girly, and just getting on with things so that I could excel at school and try to get my mother's acceptance, and therefore her love.

However, with this disconnection of self, came consequences. A paranoia, low self-esteem, eating disorders, self-harming, and in my darkest hours of feeling so utterly misunderstood, suicidal thoughts.

Unfortunately, these feelings and thoughts reared themselves again many years later, after the birth of my boys, and again later in my marriage, because I was repeating the same relationship and behaviour patterns all over again. The difference in my adult life was that I recognised that I needed to reconnect with my true self, and a long journey of healing and transformation began.

So, I invite you to take a moment and fast forward in your mind to a day in the future when your own child, now an adult, looks back and talks about whether she or he felt truly 'seen' by you.

Maybe she's talking to a spouse, a friend or a therapist – someone with whom she can be totally, brutally honest. Perhaps she's saying, 'My mum, she wasn't perfect, but I always knew she loved me just as I was.' Or, 'My dad really got me, and he was always in my corner, even when I did something wrong.' Would your child say something like that? Or would she end up talking about how her parents always wanted her to be something she wasn't, or didn't take the time to really understand her, or wanted her to act in ways that weren't authentic in order to play a particular role in the family or come across a certain way, just like I had to?

Here are some things that we can do as parents to really allow our children to be seen in their true essence, for whom they really are, and for the wonderful uniqueness they bring to enrich our world.

In fact, research and experience suggest that raising happy, healthy, flourishing kids requires parents to do just one key thing. It's not about reading all the parenting best sellers or signing your kids up for all the right activities. You don't even have to know exactly what you're doing. Just show up and

CONNECT.

Showing up means bringing your whole being - your attention and awareness - into this moment with your child. When we show up, we are **mentally and emotionally present** for our child right now. This is what I never felt I got from my mother growing up.

Longitudinal research on child development suggests that one of the best predictors for how any child turns out - in terms of happiness, social and emotional development, meaningful relationships, and even academic and career success - is having received sensitive, supportive care early in life.

Seeing our kids also means being willing to look beyond our initial assumptions and interpretations. If your child is quiet when she meets an adult, you might assume she is being impolite and try to improve her social skills. But she may simply be feeling shy or anxious. Rather than immediately correcting manners, you should first observe where she is right now, and work to understand the feelings behind the behaviour.

The point is to **develop an attitude of curiosity** rather than

immediate judgment.

You probably know the dad who pushes his disinterested son onto the football pitch, or the mum who insists her introverted child go to a drama class, regardless of the child's inclinations. These parents are failing to see who their children really are.

That sets up a despairing reality: there are some children, like I was, who live a majority of their childhoods not being seen and trying to 'please' the adults around them. Never feeling understood. Rarely having the experience that someone feels their feelings, takes on their perspective, knows their likes and dislikes. Imagine how these children feel – invisible and alone. When they think about their teachers, their peers, even their parents, one thought can run through their minds: 'They don't get me at all.' And I am testament that these debilitating thoughts can continue into adulthood.

What keeps a child from feeling seen and understood? Sometimes, it's when we see the child through a lens that has more to do with our own desires, fears, issues, and ego than with our child's individual personality, passions, and behaviour. Maybe we become fixated on a label and say, 'He's the baby,' or, 'She's the athletic (or shy or artistic) one.'

Or, 'He's stubborn, just like his dad.' When we define our kids like this, using labels or comparisons to capture and categorise them, we prevent ourselves from seeing them for who they are.

Even in our most well-meaning moments, we can fall into the trap of hoping our kids will be something other than who they really are. We might want our child to be studious or athletic or artistic or neat or achievement-oriented or something else. But what if he just doesn't care about kicking a ball into a net, or is even unable to do so? What if she has no interest in playing the flute? What if it doesn't seem important to get straight As, or it feels inauthentic to conform to gender norms?

How Can You Connect With the True You?

To live a true, purposeful, and impassioned life, we have to be connected with our soul's purpose and desires. Unless we do this, we cannot model to our children how they can live a fulfilled and successful life on their terms

Here are some simple steps you can take:

Meditation

Allow your breath to help connect your mind and body with the now. Simply taking a few deep, mindful breaths helps to lower stress levels, regulate breathing, and calm mind chatter. This is one of my favourite go-tos before a difficult conversation or task, or if I am feeling tired.

Connect with Nature

When I walk in nature, I refer to this as my 'soul food' – I feel replenished and take pleasure in knowing that I am part of something much bigger than myself. Connecting with nature brings numerous benefits – physical, mental, emotional, and spiritual – and is often easily accessible. Once this becomes part of your daily routine, you will see huge benefits, to you *and* your family.

You simply have to show up, allowing your kids to feel that you get them, and that you'll be there for them, no matter what. When you do that, you'll be teaching them how to love, and how relationships work. They'll be more likely to choose friends and partners who will see and show up for them, and they'll learn how to do it for others; they'll build skills for healthy relationships, including with their own kids, who can then pass the lesson on down the line through future generations. That's what it means to see - *really* see - your children.

Let's Reflect

Only you are here to be you.

Everyone's reality is different. Your child is not *you*.

Your greatest gift to your child is to be fully present and connected so that they are SEEN.

Your child will blossom in their own time.

Your child's uniqueness is their greatest gift to humanity.

About the Author

Clare Ford is an award-winning coach, speaker and author of *How to have a Positive and Empowering Pregnancy*, the first in the Conscious Parenting Series. Clare, a mum herself with a background in education and healing, has inspired and worked with parents and children for over 15 years. She believes in 'putting love at the heart of what matters most' - you and your family.

Her passion and specialities lie in working with families from conception onwards, to connect them with their growing babies, preparing them mentally, emotionally and spiritually for labour and the transition into parenthood, and supporting them afterwards through the ups and downs that having a family brings. Clare says, 'I have come to believe that pregnancy is a sacred journey and that birthing new life, a baby spirit that has been nurtured and nourished, by a mother who embraces the connection between mind, body and spirit, is wondrous to behold. It is my passion and calling to support women at this incredible time in their life.'

As a sought-after intuitive coach, mentor, teacher and healer, Clare regularly offers inspiring workshops and transformational in-depth coaching programmes to help clients achieve new heights of success, meaning, and spiritual aliveness. Clare is on a mission to create a ripple effect of global transformation by raising awareness of (and offering healing and mindset solutions to) mental and emotional health issues. She was finalist for Business Vision and Legacy at the MPower Awards 2018 and 2019. Having overcome emotional abuse in childhood and marriage, severe depression and anxiety and post-natal depression, she is more than qualified to walk this path in guiding others to greatness, and has spoken about this on radio, TV and various summits.

Connect with Clare:

Website: www.beautifulsouls.co.uk
Email: clareford68@gmail.com
Facebook: www.facebook.com/positiveparentingcoaching
Instagram: @beautiful50uls

Understanding the Impact of our Feelings on our Approach to Parenting

By Dave Knight

It is not the outside experience that determines our thinking and feeling. It is our thinking and feeling that determines our experience.

We all experience our own thought-created reality, moment-to-moment. As a parent, it is useful to know what is driving our behaviour, as it can steer the way that we respond to our children. In this chapter, we will be exploring how we take our experiences into parenting, for better or worse, and shape our child's experience of life. It is my hope that these words will point you towards an understanding of your own experiences so that you can bring more awareness and peace of mind into family life.

I can't think of any other time in my life when I was as proud as I was when I saw my two children born into the world.

In my eyes, being a parent is my most important role; everything else comes second best. At the time of writing, my children are young and I understand that they won't be young forever; one day they'll fly the nest. Just as we all did.

Despite their birth being my proudest moment, I experienced the first few days and weeks with each of them very differently. The first few days with our firstborn were full of fear and overwhelm. I felt clueless and ignorant to his needs when he cried. It was amazing, but extremely scary!

When our second child was born, she seemed to behave in exactly the same way, only this time I was the 'expert'. Afterall, I'd done this before (although, admittedly, changing the nappies was slightly different!). I was more relaxed, more confident, and more accepting and understanding.

There are experiences that I've had as a parent which I now realise are not only related to parenting - rather, they are feelings and fears that we carry with us as adults. When we parent, we innocently project them onto our children. This can ultimately impact on the time that we spend with them and the way that we parent.

Projecting Our Fears

I'd like to illuminate some of my own thoughts with you, as well as sharing common beliefs that friends and clients of mine have expressed over time. Perhaps these might highlight how we innocently (and yet unnecessarily) project our feelings onto our children as they grow.

Here are the common fears and worries:

- Worrying about not feeling good enough
- Having money concerns
- We should know what we want to do in life
- It's important to have a stable job/career
- We need to be interesting and fun
- 'I fell from the monkey bars at the park when I was a child and really hurt myself. There's no way I am *ever* going to let my child climb so high or do anything to hurt themselves.'
- 'I don't like spiders or any creepy crawlies. We need to stay clear of them.'
- We must have a certain body shape or image to be liked
- We need to study to a certain level to be seen as clever
- I have high expectations and need to achieve things
- No.1 is important – this is all that counts
- I hate change

- Big or tight spaces are horrible

This isn't an exhaustive list, of course. However, it may help us understand how and why we parent the way we do; what we are projecting onto our children (albeit innocently) and, of course, the impact on our children's wellbeing.

Let's take a look at three of the most prevalent beliefs and the questions we can begin to ask ourselves. Take a moment to reflect on these, or think of some other fears that you have, what you are making them mean about you, and the implications this has on how you parent.

No. 1 is all that counts

Why is No.1 important?

Where does that view come from?

If we don't achieve No. 1, does that mean we're worthless?

What level of pressure do we feel as a result of that view?

Are we putting pressure on our children to 'be the best'?

Do we want our children to feel that pressure?

We should know what we want to do in life

Why is this the case? Whose view is this and why? Is there an age by which we 'should' know this?

Who has defined that age? Is it realistic?

What do we need to put our children through for them to discover what they want to do in life? Extra study? More extra-curricular activities? And at what cost? E.g. less play, cuddles and hobbies?

'I hurt myself at the park as a child when I fell off the monkey bars. Therefore, my children will not be allowed to climb.'

Can we eliminate all danger?

What will our children miss out on?

Where does that fear of hurting ourselves stop? E.g. fear of failing, trying new things, going out the front door?

If something happened to us, will it always happen to our children?

If they demonstrate an amazing ability to climb, how will our view potentially hold them back?

When children are born, they're pure. They don't have inhibitions, judgements, opinions or biases. As they grow, they begin to see, learn, observe, reflect, hear, form habits and absorb information from the outside world - from people, what they read, and what they are told by their loved ones, friends and authority figures.

Children intellectually learn right from wrong, adopt others' viewpoints, and categorise them into 'boxes' in their brain as a way of interpreting the world around them - rather like piecing a jigsaw puzzle together so that it all makes sense. As parents, our perception of the world often becomes theirs as we attempt to impose our thoughts or reality onto them. However, once we understand where our experience of life comes from, we can begin to see that our children are creating their own reality, just as we are.

Where Your Experience of Life Comes From

In September 2018, I experienced a big insight that changed my life and created a series of 'shifts' in understanding my experience of life in so many areas -

relationships, goal setting, business – as well my understanding of stress and anxiety.

For me, the insight centred around how I was self-creating my experiences in relation to my self-identity. This insight is known as the Three Principles (Mind, Consciousness and Thought) that create all human experience. Once we understand how our experiences are self-created in one area of our lives - e.g. low mood, anxiety or stress, pressures in our job, worrying about money, insecurity in relationships - we can begin to view every area of our lives from a different perspective.

Many of us subscribe to the outside-in paradigm whereby circumstances outside of us are responsible for the way we feel. It's easy to blame our children's behaviour for our feelings of annoyance, frustration or anger, for example. However, life is inside-out. We create our experience of what is on the outside *from* the inside. We are never feeling our circumstances (or our child's behaviour); rather, we are feeling our *thinking* of our circumstances. This is why, even when we experience identical circumstances to someone else, we can each be experiencing those circumstances very differently.

The way that I parent has been significantly influenced by my grounding in the Three Principles and has allowed me to be in the moment more with my children. I now understand that my child's experiences are not permanent and change moment-to-moment. So, with the good experiences - running around with no inhibitions, being silly, singing while playing with toys, or purring with contentment when we're having a cuddle - I don't say anything. I don't ask any questions or suggest we do something together in that moment as I know that they're enjoying the moment without a care in the world.

I don't even ask, 'Are you happy?' as a way to help them capture that beautiful moment that they are in. By simply asking that question, we bring them out of the moment. Instead, I simply allow them to embrace that moment and be grateful for it.

As adults, with everything that we have going on in our lives, those periods of just being in the moment can seem fleeting. We have so much to think about – paying the bills; getting something fixed; cooking dinner; finishing some work; deadlines; or the many responsibilities and different 'hats' that we wear as parents. We may even have a tendency to make our children busy, or to fill their mind with things to think about, just because we have a busy mind.

Perhaps more pertinent is the way that we deal with the not-so-good experiences that our child is going through. It's easy to confuse our fear and panic of not wanting our child to be hurt with the love that we undoubtedly have for them. There is a huge difference between love that drives our behaviour, and behaviours that are driven by fear and panic. Naturally, love (and our desire to keep our children safe from harm) can drive our fear. It is this fear that then gets projected onto our children, influencing and driving their behaviours and experiences.

When we become aware of our thinking and how this is impacting our feelings and behaviour, we can pause, and take a different approach to the way that we respond to our children.

At 2 am one morning, after my son experienced a nightmare, we had a conversation about it. I explained how our nightmares are just thoughts that we have at night. They are no different to thoughts that we might have in the day time (or 'daymares', let's say). The only difference is that one experience is typically at night and the other occurs during the day.

On another occasion, my son experienced a friend trying to exclude him from playing a game at school. It happened to be a game that my son was particularly good at. However, his friend was trying to exclude him, which meant he couldn't play with his other friends either. When my son told me what happened, I initially felt annoyed. I wanted to come to his rescue! *How dare that boy try to exclude my son,* I thought. *I'm going to have a chat with his parents.* Fear was driving me! Then the conversation started to unfold with my son.

Me: 'Why do you think your friend was trying to exclude you from the game?'

Son: 'Well, he's worried that I might win at the game.'

Me: 'What does that show you?'

Son: 'That he didn't want to lose in front of others.'

I'm by no means suggesting that this was the perfect conversation, however, I was able to approach the conversation without fear or panic. With everything stripped back, regardless of leading my son to think of others, the conversation pointed him towards just knowing that he is OK. Have you ever heard the phrase 'there's no need to feed the rabbit'? It refers to there being no need to make something a problem when everything is OK. By not focusing my son's attention on the problem and instead redirecting the conversation to his friend, he was able to see more clearly without fear or insecure thinking clouding his judgement.

Prior to my understanding of the Three Principles and our innate health, it would have been easy to steer the conversation from a place of fear, focusing on the unfairness of it all, and making my son's friend wrong. Instead, I allowed love to lead the way.

How to Change Your Experience of Parenting

As part of my work, I also host collaborative podcasts with highly esteemed people in their field. The reason I tell you this is because I wanted to draw your attention to my collaboration that I hosted alongside some amazing women, Angela Mastwijk and Linda Spaanbroek.

Angela spoke very openly about her son and his eating disorder and how, because of her understanding of our innate health, she was able to approach that situation with her son mostly from a place of love, as opposed to being driven by her fear and panic. Her account is certainly worth listening to, which you can do via:

http://www.sundaysettler.com/collaborations

Parenting is not easy and doesn't come without challenge. That said, parenting can be an amazing experience for us. It is my most valued role in life and I can't think of anything I wouldn't do for my children for them to be content and happy.

With this in mind, here are some ideas that may help improve your experience as a parent. Please note, I'm not saying that you need to become a *better* parent, rather that you can change the way that you perceive and experience your parenting role *on the inside*. As a parent myself, I'm learning every day.

Be curious about where your experiences are coming from

Earlier in this chapter, I listed many of the fears, expectations, opinions, beliefs and judgements that we take into parenting, based upon our own experiences. Now, I want to point you towards understanding your experiences, moment-to-moment. So, if you do catch yourself feeling stressed, anxious, in a panic, overwhelmed and under pressure, or just generally in a low mood, get curious.

Ask yourself: 'Where is this experience coming from?'

Use the gift of free will to challenge your experience and realise that you have more control than you may have given yourself credit for.

Be curious about what is driving your behaviour with your children – is it from love, or is it from fear?

If you become curious about what is driving your behaviour, you create an opportunity to change the way you might parent in certain situations.

Imagine that you had a negative experience of climbing a tree as a child and now, years later, your child is an avid climber.

If you became aware that you were feeling your thinking of your child climbing a tree, rather than the actual act of them climbing the tree, what implication does this have on the way you respond to your child in those moments of fear? What would be the impact if you didn't let your own fear get in your child's way?

Whether we are behaving from a place of love or fear can be a very fine line indeed. Our love for our children is undeniable. However, be curious about the concerns, worries and fears you have that you may be projecting onto your children through your own behaviour.

Reflect – but don't be hard on yourself!

We self-create our experience in each and every moment. This means that we can respond to the *same* situation in *different* ways.

I'm sure we've all experienced our child's relentless demand for our attention: 'Daddy, Daddy, Daddy … Daddy look …

Daddy, I've got to tell you something ... Daddy, I've got to show you something ... Daddy, Daddy, Daddy!'

Most of the time, I chuckle to myself, and am able to get into the moment and be with them in the present. However, being human, there are occasions when I'm particularly busy, and hearing, 'Daddy!' every few minutes can feel incredibly distracting. 'Give me a minute!' or 'Just go and play!' I might say. And that is OK.

We are human beings. We're not supposed to be perfect. Responding in an unwanted manner by shouting or not giving our children our time happens! We shouldn't be hard on ourselves - it doesn't make us bad parents! This example merely highlights how we can experience identical situations completely differently due to our feelings in the moment. We can also be confident that whatever we are feeling in that moment will also pass.

Let's Reflect

The more we become aware of what is creating our experience moment-to-moment, the more opportunity we have to be in the present with our children. If we use our free will to become more curious about what is driving our behaviours with our children, we are in a better position to come from a place of love and clarity, instead of fear and panic.

While we have the best and most loving of intentions towards our children, by projecting our feelings onto them we can unintentionally inhibit their own progress in life as they take on our worries, opinions and pressures.

One thing that I'm deeply passionate about as a parent is allowing my children to enjoy the moment that they are in. If I have a busy mind, that is *my* busy mind, not theirs! I don't need to give my children a busy mind for the sake of it. I learn from and admire my children so much when I see them being exactly who they are – singing without a care in the world, skipping from one part of the house to another, or even daydreaming. Those moments are gold.

My only ask from you in this chapter is to observe your children, marvel at them, and learn from them when they are in that moment. You may even find yourself getting lost in it also! Be grateful for allowing yourself to be that child again with no worries. There is no need to ask them, 'Why are we so happy?' It's unnecessary thinking. Allow them to enjoy it and be grateful for it.

Likewise, there is no need to punish ourselves (or them) if we are not feeling great. This is part of who we are as human beings, and those feelings will pass.

About the Author

Dave works closely with individuals and businesses to coach them through life's challenges, gain a new perspective, and live life with more freedom.

With a background in mental health, addiction, business and sport, Dave dedicates his time to: educating people through his weekly podcast *The 9pm Sunday Settler;* collaboration podcasts with highly esteemed guests in their field; his Bulletproof Yourself Wellbeing products; 1:1 and small group coaching with clients; and by guest blogging on various sites. The focus of his work is to help people feel bulletproof against any area of challenge in their lives.

Following a number of requests from parents, Dave developed The Everyday Kids - a FREE and growing resource library for parents and children to listen, watch and read together to promote wonderful conversations and develop an understanding of our experiences as a human being. Dave sees The Everyday Kids as a lasting legacy for his children and grandchildren.

Connect with Dave:

Email: media@knights-way.com
Website: www.sundaysettler.com
Facebook: @SundaySettler and @TheEverydayKids
LinkedIn: www.linkedin.com/in/daveknight2
Instagram: www.instagram.com/sundaysettlers

Sign up to Dave's newsletter to receive updates on new products & podcast releases at www.sundaysettlers.com, or email requests for new topics to media@knights-way.com.

Be You, Be Happy

By Mark Newey

'Be who you are
Say what you feel
Because those who mind
don't matter
And those who matter
don't mind.'

~ Dr Seuss

I sat down to start writing this chapter and a thought flashed into my mind: 'Who the hell are you to write a chapter on parenting? It's too important, and you weren't great at it anyway!' And then I remembered a time, just a few years ago, when that same self-doubt reared its head. Two of my three wonderful daughters got married in 2017 and 2018. One of them was a very traditional wedding. Part of a traditional wedding is the Father of The Bride speech, which involves giving marriage advice to the newly wedded couple. 'Who the hell are you to give marriage advice? It's way too important, and you've not been great at it anyway!' However, this is a topic that I often have to explore with clients who are struggling in relationships, so I have worked out the answer…well *an* answer!

So, in my Father of The Bride speech at the wedding, I said: 'The secret to a good marriage is the ability to tell your partner *anything*. (Big Pause!) That means knowing that you're not going to be judged or ridiculed, but unconditionally supported. In other words, an open, trusting and, most importantly, authentic relationship.'

Unconditional and Authentic.

That's true of any good relationship; but in no relationship is it more important than as a parent. I certainly didn't know that during my girls' early childhood.

One of the few advantages of being an old fart (I'm 60) is that I have the experience and maybe the wisdom of two full generations of parenting: my parents of me, and me of my kids! As a therapeutic coach, I've also learnt something from every single one of my nearly 3,000 clients, including the many that are dealing with relationship, marriage, and parenting issues. So, while I wouldn't say I'm a parenting expert (actually, I'm not sure anyone can say that!), I do have a very powerful message which, if you can heed it, will transform your parenting outlook and skillset.

My Parenting Journey

I was born with very bad asthma and spent my first year of life in and out of hospital, with a 50/50 chance of survival. In those days, your parents were not allowed to stay over, so right when I should have been cuddled in my mum and dad's arms, I was on my own. I was then packed off to boarding school at the vulnerable age of seven, with severe asthma. There's no doubt that going to boarding school is a privilege

… but it's not always a pleasant one. I was terrified and, on top of that, I was bullied every night by the dormitory captain.

It took my 40+ years to work out that those two experiences led to an unconscious feeling of abandonment and a belief that I was unlovable. The word unconscious is important here because, had you asked me at any point in my life whether I felt supported, my answer would have been 'yes'…and yet …

In fact, with the recent passing of my dad, I also realised that I had little or no emotional connection with him; he wasn't capable of doing emotions. As a family, we didn't talk about anything emotional, especially things like identity or desires - we just got on with life!

This meant that I never explored who I was or what I wanted out of life. The expectation was that I would go to university and climb the corporate ladder. So, off I went, always anxious to please … and ended up with a breakdown at 40. The career was extremely stressful, partly because of regularly spending five days a week in Europe and away from home … and my family. But, more importantly, it took me another 10 years to develop a sense of self. It was immediately clear that who I am and what I thought was important in life was completely incompatible with the corporate world - a massive source of stress!

I didn't function properly for months and months and, some days, couldn't get out of bed. It was like the carpet had been pulled from underneath my feet. My girls were then 11, 8 and 4. And it was one of them that gave me the impetus to sort myself out. Antonia (4) jumped onto my bed late one afternoon and, kneeling upright in front of me, said, 'I miss you Daddy.' I thought to myself, *I've barely been out of the house, darling. How can you miss me?* Doh! I wasn't there! I may have been there physically, but emotionally I wasn't. In fact, I hadn't really been there for their whole life: I was a workaholic, and my priorities were all wrong.

I literally couldn't be more proud of my girls, but my personal parenting journey has not been at all straight-forward and is still fraught with self-doubt and self-disappointment. As a dad, it is only very recently that I've tried to be unconditional and authentic. The defining strength in the girls' growing up is undoubtedly down to their mum, my incredible wife, who is so much more than the glue that keeps the family together.

From that day forward, I developed a massive interest in the mind and how it works, gobbling up books by the dozen. I didn't go on medication but fought my way through it - I knew the problem was in my head and not 'out there'! I then got trained in coaching, NLP (Neuro-linguistic Programming), and hypnotherapy, a combination which gave me a pretty unique window into the mind. I set up my own psychotherapy practice in 2000 and have seen nearly 3,000 clients since, helping them beat stress, anxiety, and depression, and learning how to live a good and fulfilling life. I now call myself a therapeutic coach because most of my work is coaching and teaching and this has, without doubt, become my life's calling!

Authentic Parenting

The medical and educational systems are fundamentally letting our kids down. Mental wellness education would make such a massive difference to a child's mental health. It's not rocket-science, yet it's non-existent at school; it should be on the school curriculum. Having said that, much of the teaching needs to be done by you, the parents, at home. But the problem is that nobody taught us anything, either! By and large, we stumble through doing our best. I hope this chapter will make a small contribution to correct that.

My work centres on four key platforms, all of which are critical to children as they grow into adults.

Self-Awareness

Who are we? What's our personality? What are we good at? Bad at? What makes our heart sing? What do we want out of life? Can we just accept who we are, warts and all? We never really explore this stuff, and yet, how are we supposed to be happy if we don't have a solid sense of self?

The key issue here is that 91% of our mind is unconscious. In other words, 91% of how we create our reality on a moment-by-moment basis is unconscious and outside of our awareness. This is why we need to explore who we are!

Now, there are three stages to childhood:

- 0-6 years: as such, toddlers do not have a conscious mind. They can't really process, analyse, or rationalise – this is a good thing, given how much they have to learn from scratch! The problem is that they are very vulnerable as to what they do take in, and a dysfunctional family background can be really harmful in terms of what the child sees as 'normal'.

- 7-12 years: children learn principally from the adults in their life – parents, teachers, grandparents. They copy, model and normalise what you do! Again, they can very much learn the wrong things here.

- 13-18 years: the job of a teenager is to find out who they are after spending most of their life learning from you. And, of course, this is where the rebellion comes in. My belief is that you need to give your kids loads and loads of rope ... but not too much. Yes, that's an absolute nightmare!

But the more you've helped them find out who they are and accept who they are, the less rebellion you will get. However, more than ever, there's huge peer pressure for teenagers to 'fit in'. And if you try to fit in, then you change who you are, which inevitably leads to insecurity and comparing yourself constantly with others – lethal! Can you be happy being somebody else? No!

Certainly, when I was a kid, there was no conscious effort at home or at school to guide me into discovering who I was! And this is the principal reason I had the breakdown: in order to be 'successful', I had to be 'someone else'. It all came tumbling down because I should never have been in the

corporate world … not my bag at all! Funnily enough, you can be successful earning money being somebody else … but you can't be happy!

Self-Esteem

Self-esteem is the 'magic' ingredient to a happy life, and yet it is incredibly rare! Serious question: how many people in your life do you reckon are genuinely comfortable in their own skin? Most people will say out of the hundreds they know, less than five. But if we don't have self-awareness, which most of us don't, how can we feel good about ourselves?

Dr Seuss's quote at the beginning of the chapter is the answer. The problem is that we were brought up to worry about what other people think about us. In my day, it was: 'What will the neighbours say?' Actually, who cares what the neighbours think … unless they're your friends.

This is so important for the kids today because for them, social media (while it has connection benefits) creates massive pressure to be someone 'better' than they really are. But in whose eyes?

All those years ago in the corporate world, I worked out that every morning I would shut the front door or hotel room door, and I'd already got my mask on so that people couldn't see how useless, worthless, and hopeless I was. I wore a suit of armour to keep myself safe, and I'd put up a hologram of what I wanted people to see.

Most of us are doing that ... because we've been brought up to. What I didn't realise until quite recently is that I had a hologram for my boss, a different one for my colleagues, and yet another one for my friends and yes, even one for my family. Not good!

Again: can you be happy being somebody else? We need to be authentic and go out into the world without the mask, the armour, and the hologram! Your kids need to be happy with who they are, even if others think they're weird. We're all different, and diversity is something we should celebrate, not bully, shame or criticise.

The key to dropping the mask is realising how few people in your life actually matter. How many do in your life? In reality it's close family and one or two mates, the ones who would 'put their lives on the line for you'. So, for most people, it's less than 10. Nobody else matters! And yet, whose opinions do we worry about? All the people who don't matter!

This may sound like an enormous task for a parent. It's not! If you have helped your child build a sense of identity and constantly feed the message every day that they can be happy with who they are, then they will be. When they are not hiding, people will relate to them in an entirely different way. If you have no mask, people pick up pretty quickly that there's something unusually grounded about you, and how easy you are to connect with. It doesn't matter what the bully in the playground says. It doesn't matter what the manipulative cool kid says on Instagram.

Who's the one person we can't get away from? When we're happy with who we are, warts and all, life is so much easier. Stress, anxiety, and depression become what they're supposed to be: signals telling us to change how we're living right now. You can only be happy being you!

Life Vision

As you've gathered, I left school and university without knowing what I wanted out of life. It took a breakdown for me to find out what I was here for and what makes me happy. It is crazy that today kids still leave school without knowing what they want out of life.

While guidance and discussion help enormously, they have to find the answers out for themselves without pressure from their parents or teachers. Academic intelligence is only one form of intelligence, and many of us do not excel at it. While a child needs to be motivated to do their best, the pressure that many parents and the education system currently put on youngsters is insane, and guaranteed to make the child miserable. You do not need three A*s at A level to be happy!

When I visit schools, I'm always asked: 'What's your career advice, Mark?' Simple: for God's sake, do something you love. There's an old Chinese proverb that says if you do what you love, you'll never work a day in your life! If it's not going to university or training as a doctor, a solicitor, or an accountant, and not climbing the corporate ladder … that's absolutely fine. While we need to earn enough to put a roof over our head and food on the table, we do not need to be earning loads in order to lead a happy life.

At the moment, most of us hop on a treadmill and live life the way we're 'supposed' to without doing the necessary self-discovery. But, with true self-awareness and self-esteem, it's easy to find out what we want out of life. With the uncertain future that's ahead of us, kids today need to do what they love and find a way of earning from it.

Self-Empowerment

Self-empowerment is the confidence to lead a good life on our own terms, and it's essential to happiness as an adult. We need to be autonomous and self-sufficient – we learn that best as a child. The biggest barrier to this is 'helicopter parenting' which, because we (wrongly) see the world as a dangerous place, means that we 'mollycoddle' our kids.

Far too often, we insulate our children from distress and discomfort entirely. And children who don't learn to cope with distress face a rough path to adulthood. Research has established a correlation between children's anxiety and parents' behaviour. We now know that about 95 percent of parents of anxious children engage in 'accommodation': the everyday efforts we make to prevent kids' distress. Minimising things that worry them or scare them, or helping with difficult tasks rather than letting them struggle, will not help them manage it in the long term.

Despite more than a decade's evidence that helicopter parenting is counterproductive, kids today are more over-protected, more fearful of adulthood, and more in need of therapy than ever. When we shelter our kids from difficulty or challenge, we are not just shielding them from distress; we are warding off the distress that their distress causes us. More than half of children who live with an anxious parent end up meeting the criteria for an anxiety disorder themselves. The problem isn't that we aren't trying; if anything, we're trying too hard, but in ways that backfire, leaving us less time for the things that matter most.

An astounding but very revealing statistic has come to light recently: time-use studies tell us that parents today spend significantly more hours caring for children than parents did 50 years ago, despite the fact that we work more hours outside the home. It's because parents really are doing more for their kids – and many kids are doing less for themselves.

Today, only 10 percent of kids walk or bicycle to school, a massive decline from a generation ago. Forty years ago, children had regular chores in the home, but today a tiny fraction do. These activities allow a child to experience tolerating discomfort and develop a sense of personal competence and autonomy. This may be why doing chores from age three or four onwards has been found to be a very strong predictor of academic, professional, and relational success in young adulthood.

If we want to prepare our kids for difficult times, we should let them fail at things now, and allow them to encounter obstacles and to talk candidly about things that worry them. But kids who are self-aware, feel good about themselves, and know what they want out of life are almost certainly going to be self-empowered.

Let's Reflect

If you want to give your child the best start in life, there are five things you need to ensure:

Enable an open, honest, and authentic relationship where they can say *anything* to you without fear of judgement or ridicule. That also means you've got to be there for them unconditionally and without a mask yourself.

Enable them to build a solid sense of identity: of who they are.

As early as possible, give them a daily message to enable them to love who they are and not to worry what others think of them.

Help them (as early as possible) to work out what 'makes their heart sing' and, as they get older, help them create a career out of what they love.

Finally, let them fail and give them chores from a very early age, so that they can develop resilience and motivation for hard work and easily stand the knocks of life.

Resources:

- If you want to find out more about yourself (or help your teenager do the same), take a look at www.16personalities.com. It's a 10-minute questionnaire from which the resulting summary will hold up a mirror to you in terms of who you are.

- Check out Sir Ken Robinson on www.ted.com. His talk *Do schools kill creativity?* is one of the most watched TED talks with over 65 million views.

About the Author

Mark has a rare body of knowledge and practical experience based around neuro-science, which combines mental wellness (stress, anxiety and depression), leadership psychology, and life and executive coaching.

After 18 stressful years of working for corporations in international marketing, Mark set up his own training company, which was initially extremely successful, but collapsed due to a bad debt from a major client. Adding to the many years of stress, this pushed Mark over the edge, triggering a personal breakdown.

Rather than going on medication, Mark fought through his breakdown, creating a huge curiosity in the mind. This led to him training in the neurosciences and a complete career change, which has become his life's work and calling.

He set up his own psychotherapy practice in 2000 and has since helped nearly three thousand people from all walks of life - from school children through to high-flying corporate banking executives - beat stress, anxiety, depression, and lack of self-esteem and motivation.

His mission is to revolutionise the way we approach mental health with Mental Wellness Education through online programmes, businesses and schools.

Connect with Mark:

www.headucate.me for access to Mark's online Mental Wellness Programme (20 years' experience and 3000 clients encapsulated in an app!)

www.markneweymethod.com for more details on Mark and his approach.

Raising a Highly Sensitive Child

By Jen Harrison

'Highly sensitive people inhabit a world where their needs are almost universally overlooked - but simply feeling understood can be one of the most soothing things that another person can offer them.'

~ Andre Solo

Imagine living in a world where everything was 'too much' – too loud, too bright, and too busy.

Imagine not understanding the different sensations in your body and feeling uncomfortable in your own skin as you deal with the over-stimulation and sensory overload.

Imagine not being able to articulate how you feel, knowing deep down that the people that care for you don't have a clue what you're feeling, either.

Well, this isn't an imaginary world. This is the reality of living as a highly sensitive child.

In this chapter, we are going to explore what it means to be a sensitive child, and how we can adapt our parenting to embrace and nurture their sensitivity. Sensitivity isn't a burden, it's a gift, and with the right tools and parenting approach we can help our sensitive children shine their much-needed light into the world.

Growing up, I felt lost in this world. Between the ages of around 8-10, I would often say that I didn't feel well or felt sick. These two phrases became my go-to replacement for, 'I am feeling afraid or nervous,' and they stuck. I didn't have any other vocabulary back then to describe how I felt, and I can see how, as a child, I expected my parents to be able to interpret these words and understand my emotions more than I did.

Of course, this was an impossible task because they didn't understand my emotions either. Talk about frustrating for both parties! Frustrating for my parents as they couldn't understand what my feelings and words meant, and scary for me as a child because I didn't feel understood or heard.

I could speak to you all day about how that impacted my happiness as a child. In many ways, however, I am more interested in telling you about the knock on effect it had on my adult life because we spend most of our live in these latter years.

Looking back, I can see how the younger me thought that I needed to pretend to feel okay. I regularly painted a smile on my face because I believed that I needed to please people. By doing this, I pushed my feelings down and created illness in my body, often feeling anger and resentment because I believed that there was something wrong with me.

I discovered throughout my earlier years that most people don't understand emotions or know how to empathise. Back then I didn't realise that this was a lack of awareness on the part of my friends and family, and I interpreted their words and actions to mean that there was something wrong with me.

I mean, you only need to have so many people look at you with a vacant look on their face when you say that you 'don't feel well' to develop the strong belief that you are faulty, or that something about you needs to change. This is where the 'I am not good enough' belief was created for me, and boy did it stick around for a long time!

So, I spent the first half of my life feeling like I was walking around in a misty fog. I thought that was how life was supposed to be because it had become so normal to me at that point.

That was until, at the age of 31, I came across a blog on the internet about sensitivity. My eyes widened as I read the descriptions of a sensitive person, and a feeling of relief washed over me. I remember thinking, *oh, so much of this makes sense*, which was quickly followed by the thought, *and that is what has been wrong with me all of this time!* Gosh, the 'I am not good enough' wound that had been created in my childhood had stuck with me big time by that point. And I imagine that that is how you, as a parent, may also feel when you learn of this personality trait.

I know that, deep down, many of you may wonder whether this means that there is something wrong with your child and what this means for their life. I can see why you would think this. Oftentimes, the reason that you are contacting me isn't because you want to tell me all the wonderful things about your child, it's because you are really struggling, and see sensitivity as *the* thing that is causing their meltdowns and daily challenges. It really isn't the problem. Sensitivity is a beautiful characteristic to have. With it comes a real appreciation for life, a sense of creativity, and an ability to see through the window of other people's souls.

I soon came to realise for myself that being highly sensitive is simply a part of my personality. This ability to be acutely aware of my feelings caused me challenges in the earlier parts of my life because I didn't realise that, as human beings, we all need showering with love every single day. We are just like a plant that needs watering daily, come rain or shine. My parents, like most parents in this world, didn't understand what that looked like. They didn't realise that it entailed things like being mindful of their own emotions and how they were impacting me as child, communicating with me in a way that meant I felt heard by them, and helping me to name my emotions so that they didn't need to be scary, and so on.

If we want somebody to feel loved by us, it requires learning skills in order to communicate that message in a way that they feel it.

And nobody tells you this in parenting! You don't learn these life enhancing skills at school, nor do you see many books on book store shelves preparing you for this. So, it makes complete sense as to why my parents (and many other parents in the world) had no clue that the way they were interacting with me was affecting how I felt, and how I perceived the world around me.

It's essential that you are aware of these things; they're deeply important for all of your children. However, if you have a sensitive child who feels things deeply, there is a more profound importance. The knock on effect of not knowing that your son or daughter needs to feel heard and understood by you, and not realising that they need to have someone that they feel they can turn to when struggling with their emotions, really does create more fear for a sensitive child.

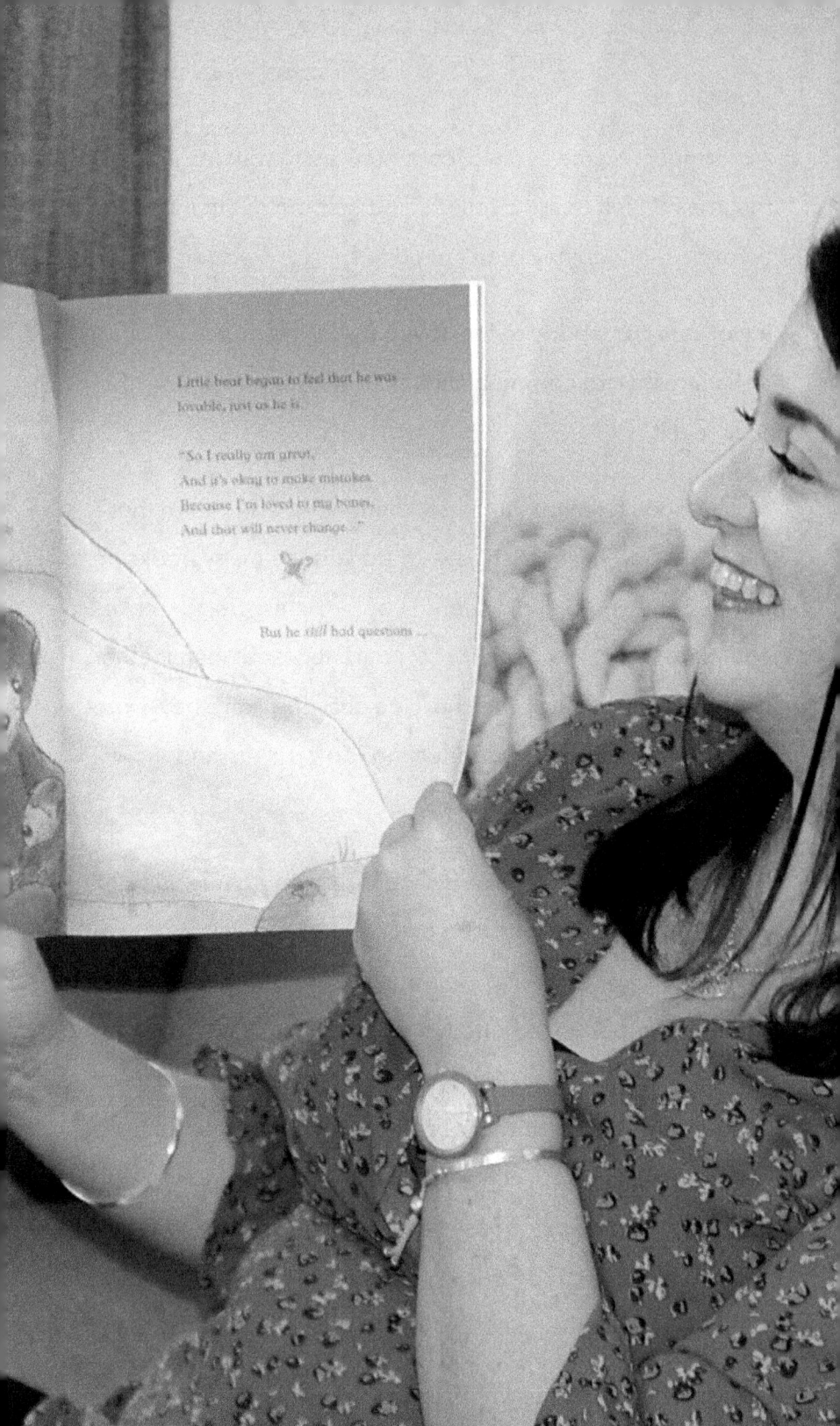

Can you imagine yourself as a child falling over, hurting your knee, and trying to tell your parents that it hurts, but all the while you are speaking Japanese and they are speaking French? Try as you might to get your message across, there would likely be a big language barrier. Eventually, you'd either give up trying, or you would start screaming and shouting.

'CAN YOU HEAR ME?!' you'd scream.

This is what your child is doing when they are having meltdowns and shouting at you. They are communicating their feelings through their behaviour. This is very common when children haven't been taught how to express their feelings with their words, and will require some 'detective' work on your part to learn how to understand what their behaviour is telling you about how your child is feeling. Much like how my parents would have benefited from knowing what I was really saying when I said, 'I don't feel well.'

If you are battling with your child's meltdowns on a daily basis, you are not alone. It is important for you to recognise, however, that you have got a huge language barrier between you. I want to help you with this because I honestly care that you both enjoy a connected and loving relationship.

You may be wondering how I came to know that all of this is important. It was through my own personal journey. I was blessed to have some people come onto my path in life who had developed an ability to empathise and hold a safe and calm space for others. As I spent time with these people, I began to learn more about why I had always felt anxious growing up, and about my emotions and how to express them in a healthy way. Soon, I began to feel like the plant (that I described earlier) was being watered on a daily basis. Let me tell you, it felt incredible! I went from feeling like a wilting lily to a bright golden sunflower.

I felt safe. I felt understood. With these basic human needs being met, I was then able to be me.

I learnt that sensitivity wasn't the problem all along. In fact, being sensitive was just a small part of who I was. The thing that had been causing me to feel in emotional pain for many years had been that I had never felt really heard, seen, or accepted in my life! Instead, I spent my formative years feeling empty, afraid, and alone in this world.

So, what does it mean to be a sensitive child?

A highly sensitive child is a perceptive soul who hears, feels, and senses things at a different frequency than other people. According to Elaine Aron, a clinical research psychologist and author who has studied high sensitivity personalities since 1990, it is thought that approximately 15-20% of people are highly sensitive. That means that approximately one in every five children are hearing and sensing their environment at a deeper level than their peers.

When you think of this in terms of a classroom of 30 children, that means that six children in the classroom perceive things deeply and are likely to be finding themselves overwhelmed by the noise, bright lights, and sensory overload that comes with a classroom and all of its decor.

I've witnessed many children with heightened emotions and deep feelings be misunderstood by those around them, and I know that, as a parent, you may struggle at times when your child seems 'different' to their siblings or peers. This is often a challenge because, understandably, you have an idea in your mind about how your child should feel or behave in life based on your own upbringing. And, when they begin to say that they don't like being in busy play centres and much prefer playing with their one friend instead of a group of children, it can make you question your parenting ability. You may even wonder whether you are giving your child all of the opportunities that you believe they should have in life.

I recall coaching one mum in England, let's call her Susie, who was experiencing these doubts herself. 'I don't want to feel like my daughter is missing out on anything in life,' she said. 'She doesn't want to go into play centres, and I worry that she will miss out on things that kids should be doing.'

The fact that her daughter was sensitive wasn't the problem here. The issue was that her mum didn't realise that what her daughter needed the most was to feel like she had some choices around going into the play centre.

Susie was so invested in her daughter having a good time that she couldn't see in those moments how she was misunderstanding her daughter's feelings.

The worst distance between two people is misunderstanding.

So, we spoke about this, and I helped Susie see how her little girl was feeling, and how she could speak to her in a way that helped her daughter feel her love and care.

What happened next was amazing! The next time her wonderful daughter said that she didn't want to be in this play-centre, Susie let her know that they could go outside for five minutes. She then calmly explained to her daughter a couple of choices that she had in that moment. Her precious daughter replied, 'I want to go back inside!'

Susie was over the moon! Can you imagine how she must have felt!? This is something that she had been battling with for a while, and all of a sudden her little girl was saying, 'Let's go back in!'

You can create deep levels of calm and assurance within your child as you learn how to communicate with him or her in ways that make them feel understood and heard by you. They need this like oxygen.

Parenting a Sensitive Child

I believe that we all have varying levels of sensitivity. It's not like some people are sensitive and others can't feel a thing. We all have the ability to perceive other's emotions.

A sensitive child is such a gift to you as a parent because they are calling you to make positive changes in your life. Just like

Susie, you can learn a lot about real connection and communication by having a sensitive child.

One of the most profound changes that you, as a parent of a highly sensitive child, can make is taking a look at your parenting style and pondering whether you could benefit by making some changes.

In my experience, having coached hundreds of people over the last ten years, I know that many of you will have experienced an authoritarian parenting style growing up, with an emphasis on obedience at the expense of your freedom to express yourself. As a result, you may really struggle to make that transition in your own parenting, until you get support with it. The reason for this is simply that you have been conditioned to parent in the way that you received parenting as a child. You may also carry some deep beliefs that authoritarian parenting is effective, or have a partner who strongly affirms this belief too.

So, let's look at this for a moment because it is really important in your quest to increase your child's self-esteem and confidence.

A sensitive child feels everything. Everything! They feel your anger and your tone. When you speak to a child with an angry tone it's designed for one thing only: to get them to act in a different way quickly. All they hear is, 'I need to change how I am behaving in this moment so that my mummy or daddy love me and stop being angry at me.'

Ohh ... wait, Jen ... can we back up a moment? Are you saying that my child doesn't feel my love and connection when I am parenting with anger on a regular basis? Yep. That is *exactly* what I'm saying. And it is really important that you see this clearly because then you are more informed about the effects of your own emotions on your child. All your child hears in those moments is your anger and your disapproval. They don't understand that those are *your* emotions and have nothing to do with them. Can you see how, in those moments when you raise your voice or shout in anger, it becomes impossible for your child to feel close to you?

This doesn't mean that you need to never feel angry. Anger is an emotion and simply a reaction to your own inner pain and feeling of helplessness in that moment. So much of how you feel today stems from your own childhood experience, so it makes perfect sense why you may have feelings of anger and anxiety yourself. In order for your child to feel deeply connected to you, you would need to find ways to address the reasons that you feel angry instead of reacting in the moment. This is lifelong work for us all, myself included! Simply throwing anger around without learning how to work through your big emotions and take ownership for them is never, ever going to lead to a connected and loving relationship with your child. Or anybody else in your home for that matter.

This is why it is important to learn how to communicate your love to your child in ways that they really feel it. These children are sensitive to your emotions and facial expressions - this includes you, your emotions, your facial expressions, the kids at school, and their school teachers.

I can easily recall my own experience as a kid at school. I can distinctively remember, even now at the age of 38, being aware of my teacher looking angry. Being around an adult who felt that way on a regular basis impacted my time at school during that year. Many of the other kids seemed really unfazed by this teacher and her levels of stress and anger. I sensed how she was feeling and, as a child who didn't know any differently, I was influenced and impacted by her feelings. I felt unsafe and afraid during that time in the classroom

When I was growing up it really was like I was speaking the emotional language of Japanese, and my parents were speaking French. This must have been really frustrating for my parents when they couldn't understand what I was saying, and it was really scary for me as a child when the adults around me didn't understand what it was that I was trying to communicate to them.

This is why it's super important, as a parent, to be able to meet your child where they are at. This means learning to understand their language – what makes them feel loved by you, and what their behaviour means.

Having this understanding can be a great advantage to you in everyday life. Let's take a look at days out, for example. For your highly sensitive child, an outing can sometimes be an overwhelming sensory experience. Other babies may handle being passed from person to person just fine. Not your little guy – he gets overwhelmed and fussy. He often needs 'down time' after play dates to restore his emotional balance, and is only calm enough to eat when his environment is quiet and relaxed. Highly sensitive babies can often have difficulty relaxing enough to fall asleep, requiring hours of holding, rocking, and bouncing – it's the only thing that works!

For an older child, a day out that looks fun to you can be a jam packed day of sensory overload, leaving them feeling emotionally wired, in tears, and having meltdowns while you wonder, 'What just happened? This was supposed to be a fun filled day and you are in tears…'

In these moments, it's key to be mindful of how sensitive your child may be to their environment. I often recommend to parents to create 'pockets of peace' during the day. This means that, if you do have a fun day planned, have a think about how you could implement small breaks throughout the day. This might look like taking time out to have a picnic in a quiet area or outside under a tree. You could encourage your children to sit down and eat, play some gentle music on your smartphone, and let them know that this is your pocket of peace time, telling them that, in twenty minutes, you will all go back in to the play-centre/play in the park etc. These kids don't know that they need this quiet time to restore their balance, so it is down to you as the parent to be aware of this ahead of time and plan it in. Trust me, you will be thankful that you did this when it gets to the end of your day and your child is more likely to settle to sleep because they haven't just spent their day being overstimulated.

Top Three Tips to Raising a Highly Sensitive Child

I know that quick tips can be really helpful to you as a busy parent who is keen to learn, so I am going to run through three of my best behavioural changing strategies for raising your sensitive child.

Name your child's feelings for them, or at least invite them into the conversation about feelings. This isn't about putting words into their mouth and telling them how they feel. It's more about giving them the opportunity to feel seen and heard by you, and learn to identify those feelings which will, in turn, help them to feel more empowered and in control of their emotions

So, one way that you could do this would be to say something like, 'It looks like you are feeling sad right now, Harry.'

A simple sentence like this is firstly an expression of love and care - you're letting your child know that you notice how they feel. Secondly, it's a sign of acceptance - you aren't judging their feeling . And thirdly, you are helping them by giving a name to that feeling that they're likely experiencing.

Learn to self-regulate. If you experience stress and anger on a consistent basis at the moment, your son or daughter knows this and feels it. They are sensitive to emotions. You really can't hide it from them either, as annoying as that is. One mum in New York that I coached recently shared this when she learnt how her son picked up on everything: 'I feel like he's a little detective watching my every move!'

When it comes to your own stress levels, you need to recognise that you simply can't pour from an empty cup.

So, what can you do to take care of your own well-being? Ask for support, and allow yourself to receive support and love from another person. I understand why you may find this difficult if you didn't have that modelled to you when you were growing up. It's pretty difficult to shake that off overnight. But shake it off you must, if you want to be present enough to be able pass calm, peace, and love onto your child. This is essential for your own happiness too!

So, as you begin to feel that your cup is overflowing more, you then have more love to give to your child. You may have viewed love as something that you automatically just feel and give to your child, as I used to believe. However, I came to learn that it doesn't work like that. Love is an action. Love isn't just a thought or a feeling. Sure, we can love someone. But what use is it if the other person doesn't feel it?

We can stand here and say, 'I love you,' until the cows come home. But if the other person feels something very different coming from us, then we have to take a step back and ask ourselves, 'Am I expressing love to my child in a way that he or she feels it?'

And oftentimes, we really aren't. We are doing our best one hundred percent of the time. It's just that there's room for improvement and learning. And that's okay! You will know if your child isn't feeling connected to you by the way that they feel - if they feel angry or anxious on a regular basis, there is work to do here between the two of you.

Please don't think that this means you're failing as a parent. This is the trap that I hear many parents fall into. I hear many mums and dads say to me that they feel like they aren't doing a good job, and are scared of ruining their child's life when they begin to learn the impact that their words are having on their children.

Do you relate to this? Do you ever feel like you need to 'get it right' in your parenting, or that you aren't good enough? You are not alone if you do. The thing is, this just isn't true! Parenting doesn't come with a guide book, and there are always new things to learn about another little human being.

Consider the words and tone that you use when you speak to your child. Oftentimes, when we are in a rush or feeling stressed, we say things in a way that hurts the other person, without intention or even realising it. This is important to understand as a parent to a highly sensitive child – these emotions are felt deeply by them; they will take to heart everything that you say, and it will impact how they feel.

Take, for example, the school mornings when everyone is in a mad rush to get out of the door and to school on time. Let's suppose that your child runs upstairs to get their PE kit at the last minute, and you're stood there looking at your watch thinking, *great! That's another day where she's going to be late. I hate these school mornings, they never go to plan.*

It's very likely that the next words that come out of your mouth will be filled with even the slightest tinge of anger; whether that be in your tone, your words, or both. What can you do to resolve this?

Tell them the truth about how you spoke to them. Own it.

This is such a humbling experience. As the adult who wants to give the impression that we are right all of the time, it's not always easy to say to a child, 'Hey, I messed up and I was wrong.' Try it though! I can't tell you the amount of mums that I speak to who say to me, 'If my parents told me that they'd made mistakes or apologised to me, it would have made such a difference to me!' You have the power and the opportunity to offer that same gift to your child today.

So, how could you do this?

Like this:

'Harry, this morning before school I shouted at you and got angry. That was my mistake. You wouldn't have felt loved by me in that moment. Anger is never the best way to speak to somebody.'

The words 'I love you' get thrown around so much but they really mean nothing when they aren't backed up by loving actions – highly sensitive children know this!

So, what can you do differently to express love to your child in a way that they will feel it?

Firstly, ask your child how they feel your love. Oooh! I can hear light bulbs going off here in your mind as we speak. Have you ever considered that you can ask your child something like, 'When do you feel most loved by me?'

Or, 'When did you feel closest to me this week?'

Or, try this one on for size: 'Has there been a time this week where you didn't feel relaxed or close to me?'

When you ask for feedback, putting yourself in a vulnerable position to hear something that you may not like, you gain powerful knowledge of how to better connect with your child. This way, it becomes a two-way conversation, rather than simply trying to love somebody and hoping that it's sticking. When asking for feedback the truth might sting a little, but it's for the greater good for you and your family.

And lastly, here's a bonus tip for you …

Don't try to change or mould your child into who you believe they need to be, to fit in.

Love and embrace them for exactly who they are! In a world of conflict and chaos we need more kind, compassionate, and sensitive souls!

Let's Reflect

A highly sensitive child is highly perceptive who feels and senses things at a different frequency than others. It is thought by clinical psychologist Elaine Aron, that 15-20% of the population are highly sensitive. That gives you some indication as to how many sensitive children may be in your child's class.

As you learn how to name feelings and support your child in this process too, they will feel your emotional presence and be better equipped to self-regulate when they feel anxious. Naming feelings is a powerful way to manage your emotions.

Your parenting style greatly impacts how your child feels, and it is really important to move on from the ways that you were parented and embrace a more effective style. Authoritarian parenting styles just won't cut it for young people, especially sensitive children who feel so deeply.

The more that you learn how to self-regulate and better understand your own emotions, the greater capacity you have to be emotionally in tune with your child. They will greatly thank you for this – trust me! And you will benefit from feeling that peace too!

The words and tone that you use with your child will impact how confident and calm they feel. When you forget this (because you will if you're human), it's important to remember that there is a way to repair that. Simply own your emotions and reactions, and communicate that to your child so that they feel your love.

About the Author

Jen Harrison is a children's author and family relationships expert, with over ten years of experience coaching almost 1,000 parents globally, and successfully helping them to improve their lives at home within a matter of weeks.

She has featured in British magazines as a parenting advice expert and as an in-house coach for the online children's growth mindset company *Big Life Journal*.

Jen has been named 'The Child Whisperer' by mums worldwide and has been highly rated by famous American actress, L A Baker, who played Ellen in Will and Grace. Jen has a proven track record for showing mums how to reduce their child's anger and anxiety by 80% within six weeks or less.

Jen is also the author of the bestselling children's book *Just As You Are,* and loves writing and playing on the beach or in nature when she is not coaching mums over Zoom or FaceTime.

Connect with Jen:

Website: www.sensitivechild.co.uk
Instagram: @thehighlysensitivechild
Facebook: Supporting Sensitive Children

Want to know how to bring more calm into your home? Visit Jen's website to sign up to her FREE training!

Just As You Are: Celebrating the Wonder of Unconditional Love is available from Amazon, Barnes & Noble, and Waterstones.

Rewards, Consequences, and Praise: Why Are They Wolves in Sheep's Clothing?

By Jane Evans

'When a child can't calm down, they need connection and comfort, not criticism and control.'

~ Jane Evans

Before we dive into rewards, consequences and praise, let's be clear about one very important thing...*YOU are your child's best resource.* In fact, two very important things...*Your child is totally in love with you.*

Thus far in your journey as a parent or carer, you may never have had the opportunity to truly explore rewards, consequences, and praise in the way you are about to. This makes you very normal indeed.

Most parents, carers, and many professionals use rewards, consequences, and praise on a daily basis. And, realistically, a form of rewarding, punishing, and praising children's behaviours has been handed on from generation to generation. So how could and would you know any differently? It's important to resist the urge to beat yourself up in any way, shape, or form if you've been dipping in and out of using rewards, consequences, and praise! Pretty much everyone has, including me.

As Maya Angelou says,

'Do the best you can until you know better. Then when you know better, do better.'

Being curious, learning, and applying new knowledge and understanding has been my journey as a parent and as a professional – and I hope it's now yours too.

Why am I calling rewards, consequences, and even praise wolves in sheep's clothing?

The short answer is because rewards, consequences, and praise can seem so harmless, familiar, and pretty inoffensive, a bit like a sheep. Unless, that is, you look under their woolly exterior! Then it's possible to see the wolf with its big teeth and sharp claws. This is a *wolf* which may harm you, your child, and the amazing lifelong relationship you are very keen to nurture with them.

A few familiar myths about rewards, consequences, and praise that serve no child or parent:

1. Adult life is all about rewards, consequences, and praise
2. Children love rewards and lap up praise
3. Children soon learn from a negative consequence
4. Rewards and praise are 'positive parenting'

Why on earth would you get rid of rewards?

Rewards can be anything you use as a way to get your child to do, or not do, something. The reward will be something you know they like or will enjoy. It could be extra screen-time, sweets or candy, an outing, a toy – anything you know that brings them pleasure.

Rewards are mostly defined and agreed upon in advance, such as using a system, e.g. a sticker chart, or a marble in the jar, or something else visual. The whole reward/bribery process hinges on a child grasping that, if they do what you want them to, they can 'earn' something they like, love, or crave.

Rewards are not connecting, respectful,l and accepting of the whole child.

My son, who is now grown up, still reminds me of the hugely desirable Spiderman compact he was desperate to have (it was cool, to be fair). I bribed him with it to try and get him to sleep a whole flipping night in his own bed! He was six at the time, and I was keen/desperate for this to happen. So much so, that I completely failed to be curious about why it was so hard for him to sleep the whole night alone in his own bed.

Instead, I decided he could do it if the prize was big enough.

Bribing him to do stuff was a real mismatch for how we generally got along. It disrupted the trust and respect in our relationship. I stuck a chart on his wall, we miserably went through it … and he has never forgotten it! Probably because, on some level, he sensed that this system was not respecting him, his needs, and how we normally treated each other.

Why I Would Never Use Rewards Now

Over twenty years ago, I did not know what I'm crystal clear about now! Namely that, rewards are about control. When I used the much-desired Spiderman compact as a reward to modify behaviour, I was gaining control and compliance over my child who was dependent on me for his comfort and safety.

I unintentionally gave him a powerful message that my love and acceptance of him hinged on him keeping me happy by staying in his bed. Whereas my message should have been that he could always come to me any time he felt scared, was unsettled, and in need of my comfort. Pretty stupid of me, even potentially dangerous.

Ultimately, when you choose (as I did) to rely on rewards as a way of getting children to do what you want, it puts a real barrier between you and them. Why? Because rewards introduce conditions into your relationship with your child. They soon pick up that life is better when they are pleasing you and are 'in your good books'.

What you want, and they need, is for your child to come to you in any situation – with the good, not so good, and wobbly indefinable bits of being a child, teenager, and adult. That's the safest, healthiest kind of relationship for a child to rest in.

If children grow up being rewarded for pleasing those who are ultimately in charge of them, it introduces an unhelpful uncertainty – *have I gotten this wrong? Will they be unhappy with me?*

Rewards increase vulnerability

Babies and children are brilliantly and efficiently wired to seek connection with the main adults in their daily lives, as it's nurturing and life preserving. The connection they need should be freely available. In fact, the more it is, the less they will demand it. Connection creates inner safety and calmness. Using conditions, such as rewards and consequences, makes this free-flowing connection messy as its certainty gets mixed in with earning stickers, smiley faces, and trying to get stuff right!

Rewards bring in the concept that 'pleasing the grown-ups' means life feels better, even safer. Each time your child gets the pleasure of the treat, and a dose of seeing and feeling you are happy with them, they get wired to focus on that, and learn to ignore their feelings and needs.

Through repetition, your child's brain, nervous system, and internal body chemistry learn – *when I please those I'm in love with, and dependent on, it fills me with feel-good chemicals. I feel safe, calm, contented, and emotionally seen.* Sound good? Well, this wiring and internal chemistry may get your child to conform, as it feels better for them. But is this the healthiest, safest way to prepare your child for life?

Rewards and consequences are great if your focus is on training your child to keep you happy, and to comply with your wishes and needs. But will such compliance and a focus on keeping others happy nurture their emotional, psychological, relational, and physical needs, safety, and wellbeing?

If a child becomes wired to feel better when keeping others happy, especially those in any position of power over them (which is pretty much all adults), if your child learns to get connection with adults by sticking to rules and fulfilling the adult's wishes and needs, they will try to do this if they can. And, as uncomfortable as this might be, anyone who is a threat to your child in *any* way will pick up on this, and slowly - carefully - use it to get what they want from your precious child.

Alfie Kohn, thought leader and the author of *Unconditional Parenting* (Atria Books, 2005), and of many other books on the use of rewards and competition, says:

'Children need to be loved as they are, and for who they are. When that happens, they can accept themselves as fundamentally good people, even when they screw up or fall short. And with this basic need met, they're also freer to accept (and help) other people. Unconditional love, in short, is what children require in order to flourish.'

Rewards create confusion

If children pick up early on that keeping you onside and pleased with them is the best outcome, then what will happen when they are struggling to say no to pressure from their peers? Maybe pressure to skip school, try alcohol, or jump in a car when their intuition is saying don't!

If, at mealtimes, a child has to force their veggies down or clear their plate despite feeling full, so as to get the smiley sticker on the chart, will they ever enjoy sitting down and eating with you as they get older?

If someone befriends a child in real life (or online) using a mix of rewards, praise, and threats, you don't want this to subconsciously feel familiar to them so that they go along with it. You need this system and manipulative energy to feel at odds with how they've experienced relationships. Then, they're much more likely to tell you. I don't mean to scare you … actually, I do! Because ultimately, using rewards could increase your child's vulnerability.

Random rewards are better, aren't they?

Now, random rewards are 'tricky sheep'! I was a big fan of random rewarding, as I felt my son didn't have to earn them, and his delight at a random reward was very clear which was satisfying for me too. But, of course, I was still the one with the power over what he got, when he got it, and why.

You might choose to give your child a random reward for using their potty, doing well in a test, sitting 'nicely' for a meal out, or anything that keeps you happy and you're keen to encourage more of.

The random reward is a way of flagging up – *YES this is it! I want you to do this behaviour as it makes you more likeable to me and the rest of the world.* Wanting to clearly define these desirable behaviours makes you human. After all, we've all endured that shaming look from some tight-lipped person in the supermarket when our child is flailing on the floor in a state of protest and distress!

Q. What can you replace rewards with? I will definitely tell you at the end!

Are consequences the evil twin sheep of praise?

Consequences are a bit trickier to nail down. Firstly, there are *agreed consequences*. These are the ones you might love to think of as the most rational ones. After all, you have talked about them with your child, who seemed to understand, and may even have agreed to them.

What a relief – now you don't need to feel bad if they 'choose' to do the thing that will bring them the *agreed consequence*! Being rational can seem like such a great 'get out of gaol guilt-free' card for any parent! But, ask yourself this: how much does using consequences nurture safe, unconditional acceptance and connection in your relationship with your child? Will they feel safe enough to come to you if they feel they've got something wrong?

How I Stuffed up, Again!

As a childminder, I made a right old dog's breakfast of using consequences! By this time, I was trying even harder not to be mean to children. But there was a part of me that felt the children I was caring for might sometimes need a space to *calm down and reflect* if things had gone wrong.

I decided the stairs could be the 'calm down zone'. I didn't see this as a consequence but, of course, the children did, especially poor Alicia. She spent the most time 'calming down' as she often struggled to play with the other children.

Her outbursts could be pretty explosive, and I was keen to teach her how to come back from them, and also to protect the other children from her seeming fury.

What I failed to see was how shaming it was for Alicia to be encouraged to go away from the others when she was struggling with too many feelings, and flicking into fight/flight a great deal of the time. Ultimately, the 'calm down zone' was a consequence for her big feelings. Alicia knew it and, deep down, I and the other children did too.

Agreed consequences may look like this:

- If you don't eat your main meal - you won't get desert
- Every time you leave your shoes in the middle of the hall - you lose 10 minutes screen time (as it's on the chart/agreement you signed!)
- If you get out of bed before the agreed time - you lose 5-minutes in the park
- Three red cards from school - you won't go to Caz's party
- Forget your school books three times - no pizza night
- Fail to load the dishwasher - lose the weekly allowance

Natural consequences are fine, surely?

Then there are the seemingly innocent looking **natural consequences**, which are seen as a kinder way of teaching children. After all, adult life is full of consequences so it's best to learn this early on.

If you leave the keys in your car door, it'll be gone when you come back. If you overspend, you'll run out of money. Upset your boss and you'll lose your job. But are any of these really true most of the time? … No!

Leave your keys and someone will likely run after you and tell you. Overspend and all too often the bank will increase your overdraft. Upset your boss and, in many cases, they can't sack you on the spot.

Of course, sometimes life does dish up consequences. But, ironically, trying to avoid them creates anxiety for so many of us. Whereas, being calmer and more present in life pretty much ensures that there are few negative consequences, and that sorting them out is pretty easy. Which is EXACTLY what we want for your children!

My final thought on *natural consequences* is that they are just plain mean. The best *meanness test* is to ask yourself, 'Does this *natural consequence* I am allowing to unfold for my child feel, look, or sound kind? Would I let it happen to an adult I adore?'

Children and teenagers are forgetful. They have hugely underdeveloped brains, and are wonderfully designed to live in the moment, and generally be in a state of wonder at the world around them. So, do we need to punish them for that?

- Forget your school books – take the punishment school hands out
- Fail to bring your favourite top down to be washed – go without it for the outing
- Ignore requests to come down for dinner – have cold food to eat
- Refuse to put your coat on – get wet and cold
- Not come when you are called – miss a FaceTime with Grandma

One last thought on consequences is about the *randomly out of the blue consequences*. These are often the meanest, most toxic ones, and happen when you are very tired, emotionally empty, and stressed. So, you go off at the deep end and suddenly declare:

'Right, that's it ...'

'No more sweets/candy for the rest of the month.'

'You are grounded for the next 2 weeks.'

'Jake is not coming round for the rest of the holidays.'

'No more screen time during the week, at all, ever.'

'I'm putting all your toys in a bin bag and you won't get them back.'

'You are not coming with us to the zoo this weekend.'

Q. So how will children learn what they need to do? Honestly, trust me, I will ALSO cover this at the end!

Please don't take away praise!

How the hell can praise possibly be, in any way, shape or form, harmful to your child or your relationship with them? After all, *everyone* likes praise, don't they? In fact, it's a great motivator, surely?

OK, so I challenge you to run out into the street now and bring me an adult who can easily, and peacefully, accept your praise. What you will most likely get is an uncomfortable rejection of what you've offered as praise, or a convincing counter argument, or they'll simply change the subject. This is because it feels yucky unless they have grown up with a different form of praise (also coming at the end, I promise!).

Praise can be something a child comes to expect, as it was part of the big fuss over the poo in the potty years ago.

A child discovers that if they do well in their spellings – *I am so proud of you getting 9/10 for your spellings, you did so well!*

For reaching a target – *I am so pleased you kept your room tidy all week.*

Following an instruction – *You did so well to remember to bring your letter and your sports kit home from school, I'm so happy you did.*

Showing kindness – *You were so kind to Anna; I am so proud of you.*

Winning a sports event – *Wow, you are so amazing! Well done! Let's tell Grandad how well you did.*

Don't get me wrong – parental praise can be a motivator and, in the moment, it might feel good. But is it really about the child? Or is it back to your need to plant that damn flag again? The YES, this is it! *I want you to do this behaviour as it makes you more likeable to me and the rest of the world* flag!

Let's Unpick the Core Aim of Rewards, Consequences, and Praise

Rewards are bribes. These say to a child, *'Do what I want you to and I will give you something you really like and want. You will need to comply to my wishes, as I am the gatekeeper to the thing you want. Oh, and I will decide if and when you get it!'* However, your child will also need to read the small print on rewards to get the full picture!

Dear Much Beloved Child,

Please note:

There will be times I may forget to give you the reward as I'm so busy and tired.

Or I will give it begrudgingly as I don't really feel you should have it because, although technically you have complied enough, you also annoyed me over something else. So, your reward will come smothered in my inner resentment.

Also, there will be times when I am fully fed-up, and you just won't get it anyway!

Signed: Your otherwise very loving parent.

* * *

Essentially, consequences exist to get children to do or not do things. Consequences are used to cause a child emotional, mental, and sometimes physical discomfort, distress, and even pain, so that, over time (sooner rather than later), a child will change their behaviour to meet an adult's expectations and wishes.

To be fair, years ago, B.F. Skinner developed operant conditioning by studying animals in boxes and using ways to reward them with food, or shock them with electricity. They did learn! But is this really what you want in the relationship you are growing with your child?

Modifying children's behaviour can seem like responsible parenting or caregiving. After all, how will they learn unless adults are using rewards and consequences to clearly highlight *do more of this, and less of that?*

As for using praise, sit in the uncomfortable place of it being more about your needs than about your child's.

What the Hell Can You Do Instead?

Thanks for waiting until the end. Let's revisit the two very important things…

YOU are your child's best resource.

Your child is totally in love with you.

Which means your responses and reactions are very powerful indeed. In the first seven years of a child's life, they are in *receive mode* and learn from watching, listening, and sensing how to be a human being. So, how you are with them and around them is everything. It shapes their belief system, self-worth, and fight/flight/freeze/befriend response for life.

What they need from you is always the same - calmness, safety, connection, and compassion. Yes, even if they've pushed their brother over for the 6th time today. Yes, even if they've called you a 'poo head' and stomped upstairs, slamming their bedroom door. Yes, even if they've scraped the whole side of your car by not parking it where you told them to.

So, instead of rewards, consequences, and praise, they need you to do this:

Check in - with yourself, as they've not put their shoes away AGAIN!

Calm - yourself and them, if they are stressed.

Connect - with yourself and them, rather than diving into the behaviour or task.

'How's your programme/day been? (LISTEN) Thanks for letting me know. I noticed your shoes aren't quite on the rack yet, could you pop them on there, please?'

Curiosity - whatever feelings they then show, breathe. You need to be authentically curious about how they are feeling. 'Are you OK? You seem a bit cross about the shoes ... [PAUSE and LISTEN].'

Co-operation – it turns out they don't want to come away from the TV to put their shoes on the rack. Fair enough ... would you?

Be curious about how to make this easier for them – what can you do? They might say, 'Put my shoes on the rack, please.' So, why not do it?!

After all, you've had a chat about the need for shoes to be on it. They get it, but because they rushed in the door, they forgot. Luckily, this kind, calm, conversation where their views and feelings mattered attaches a wonderful bunch of emotions to the next time they come in and need to put their shoes away!

Sound a bit long winded? At first, it is. All the parents I coach ask me for the short version to easily remember. It goes like this:

> 'Unless and until you can respond to your child with kindness, connection, and compassion, keep still and be quiet!'

Simple but NOT easy. But, this reliance on a respectful, compassionate relationship is an amazing way of being present in your child's life. It's full of teaching, respect, kindness, feelings, connection, safety, and fun. The more you make this a way of *being* and responding to your child, rather than *doing* to your child so as to get them to behave, it will change everything and give you the amazing relationship you and your child need and deserve now, and for the rest of your lives together.

Let's Reflect

Rewards are not connecting, respectful, and accepting of the whole child.

Rewards are used to gain control and compliance over a child who is dependent on their care giver for comfort and safety.

Children and teenagers are forgetful. They have hugely underdeveloped brains, and are designed to live in the moment - do we need to punish them for that?

Consequences are about the parent, not the child, and the need to change a child's behaviour to meet an adult's expectations and wishes.

And remember ... your child is totally in love with you! They need you to be their safe, kind, compassionate, and connected place!

About the Author

International parenting coach, childhood anxiety and media expert, Jane Evans credits the children, young people, parents, and carers she worked with and cared for as being her greatest teachers. They have consistently shown and taught her the realities of how lives are profoundly shaped by early childhood experiences.

Jane's huge curiosity about the *why* behind children and adults' struggles with anxiety and low self-worth has led her to study a wide range of cutting-edge body and brain-based science.

Jane brings her knowledge, her professional and life experience into her roles as a renowned TV and radio expert, author of four children's' books, her TED Talk, and her international speaking and coaching. She makes the *why* behind people's behaviours simple to grasp, and provides solid, practical solutions so everyone has the opportunity to live well beyond their anxiety, and other limiting beliefs and behaviours.

Connect with Jane:

Website: www.thejaneevans.com/parenting-beyond-anxiet-to-peaceful-connection-programme

Facebook: Parenting Children Beyond Anxiety

TED Talk: Taming and Tending Your Meerkat Brain

Email: jane@thejaneevans.com

Children's Books (available on Amazon)

Little Meerkat's Big Panic: A Story About Learning New Ways to Feel Calm

How Are You Feeling Today Baby Bear?: Exploring Big Feelings After Living in a Stormy Home

Kit Kitten and the Topsy-Turvy Feelings: A Story About Parents Who Aren't Always Able to Care

How to Calm the Storm in an Angry Child

By Rachel Devereux

'You are one thought away from happiness, one thought away from sadness. The secret lies in thought.'

~ Sydney Banks

It's really tough when kids hit out in rage. They get so caught up in the moment that many parents struggle with how to contain them! Tantrums begin at around 18 months, the development of their wants and perceived needs outweighing their communication skills which leads to extra frustration. When parenting a toddler, it's easier to remain calm, to wait out their storm. But as our children grow and their outbursts become more aggressive and forceful, how do we keep our cool and let them know it's all OK?

We can try to stamp out their anger and send them to their room, sit on the naughty step or take away their toys. Withholding love, deprivation of liberty, or forcible isolation might be other ways to describe these punishments. Time-out is actually an abbreviation from psychological studies in the 50s and 60s called 'Time out from Positive Reinforcement'. What started with pigeons and chimpanzee behaviour modification was carried through into children's behaviour modification.

But this actually teaches them a lesson we don't intend.

It basically tells a child that those behaviours are 'bad' and 'I can't deal with them'. So, how can they possibly learn to manage their anger if you can't? Alfie Kohn, lecturer in the areas of education, parenting, and human behaviour, goes on to explain that love withdrawal causes an emotional pain, which is just as effective in the short term as physical pain, but with longer lasting effects.

Sorry for the truth bomb here. You're their parent and I know you can deal with everything - the good, the bad, and the ugly. And some days, when we're being really honest with ourselves, we have to admit that our children are little mirrors of us - which makes it all the harder to deal with!

Sending a child away doesn't give them time to think about what they have done; it gives them time to stew and increase their anger - to redirect it at you, or to work out how to do the action again and not get caught. Or, they may fear the consequences and not do it again, giving the impression that their punishment has been effective. But how about nurturing a strong moral compass in a child and for them to make choices later on in life based on what is right or wrong, rather than the fear of getting caught? Punishment, extraction, or removal of belongings creates a feeling that is hard for the child to deal with, and can lead to more negative connotations. I know this from experience. And countless psychological studies have shown that punishment only works long-term if it is serious enough to pain and hinder you for a lengthy time (and thus increasing the likelihood of psychological issues later on in life), or the punisher is present at the time of the crime. A five-minute time out doesn't change the behaviour, which is why it's used repeatedly for the same offence.

No Bad Emotions

It's important to let young children be at peace with all of their emotions. Feeling sad, angry, and worried are just feelings – they are neutral. As are calm, at peace, and free. As are happy, excited, and giddy. They simply arise from thoughts in that moment. A happy thought can lead to a happy feeling, while a sad thought may lead to a sad feeling, and so on. Thoughts are neutral, until we attach meaning to them. By telling our children to stop crying or to stop being angry, for example, and thus encouraging them to deny those emotions, we are saying that some are bad and some are good. Our children hear, 'I only love you when you're happy and pleasantly behaved.'

Children see the world through children's eyes. The things that make them happy (farts) or sad (being told no chocolate before dinner) are not necessarily the things that we, as adults, would feel happy or sad about - personally, I think farts can be funny, but I may be on my own here! The point is, all of their feelings are valid, even if we cannot make sense of them through our own (and very adult) lens.

Storms

I think of emotions like weather - sometimes it's sunny, sometimes it's cloudy, and sometimes there's a full-on storm raging. I can't do anything to change the weather, only prepare myself for it. And in England, we can have four seasons in one day!

'There's no such thing as bad weather - only unsuitable clothes.' ~ Alfred Wainwright (also credited to Scandinavian folklore)

Well, I would say, 'There's no such thing as bad emotions, only ineffective ways of dealing with them.' Trying to change people's emotions or to never have bad days is like trying to push rain back into the clouds. A good storm can be perfect for clearing the air, feeding a dry landscape, and creating space for something new.

Unconditional Love

Our children deserve to be loved unconditionally, warts and all. I want my child to be a well-rounded adult that cares for other people's wellbeing, as well as his own. I want him to be emotionally stable and able to navigate the harshness of the real world with a smile on his face. I want him to be free to take risks and try something new knowing that, no matter what happens, I will always love him … including taking him cookies in prison, if necessary (although I'm hoping it won't come to that!).

I say this because we all mess up! We all do something without thought that causes upset to others. Sometimes, what seems like a perfect thing to do is actually the worst thing ever! Sometimes, people make the wrong choices, despite knowing the risks, and land in jail. Would I disown my child? No, probably not. I know a man who has gone to jail for attempted murder. His mum still loves him, she wants the best for him, *and* she knows he needs the punishment and rehabilitation of incarceration. She really might not like him, but she's still his mum and wants him to get better.

How to Handle Angry Outbursts in Your Child

It's easy to fall into patterns of withholding love, or punishing the emotions when our children have angry outbursts. It has been our default for many generations; few of us learned how to express anger healthily or how to be at peace with all of our emotions. Now, with this new awareness, we can choose a different way.

Here are some tried-and-tested approaches that I have personally used when my children lash out.

Shouty Anger: Waiting it Out

I give some examples of phrases to use here when your children start shouting in anger. The important thing is not the phrase, but rather to be in a calm frame of mind, and mean what you say. Children feel your energy, their nervous system is co-regulating with yours, so they will know if you mean what you say, or not. The words are merely vessels for your feelings – use ones that feel right for the moment. The key here is to validate their feelings and experience.

'I see you're feeling angry right now.'

'It's hard for us to discuss why you're so upset when you're shouting.'

'It's hard for me to hear clearly when you shout.'

'I'm right here for you when you're ready to talk.'

Waiting it out can often be the most successful diffuser. Be at peace with their anger – discussions come later.

Keeping calm and present is the most important thing here. And it's OK to explain that dinner needs to be made, for example, and that they can come and speak to you in the kitchen when they're ready.

Hitting Anger: Holding

My children are used to being touched, hugged and carried in tight slings. So, for them, comfort comes in security of tight hugs. This can be helpful for them – but sometimes exacerbates their anger. It's important to read the situation individually each time and be prepared to ditch this approach.

Holding your child in a bear hug, while remaining calm and not getting angry with them, can show them your love while they fizzle out. My three-year-old, when overtired, needs this.

Otherwise, giving her space enables her to become more overtired and destructive – if she chooses to move away and not hit me or break things, then that is fine too.

Holding hands and feet so that they can't hit you, while reinforcing that you don't want to be hit, can be helpful. If they're screaming 'let me go' then, of course, I will; if they hit me, I will need to stop them.

Hitting can be redirected at sofa's or pillows.

'I see you're feeling angry and needing to hit, let's hit this pillow instead.' This usually gets my son so giggly that the anger disappears. We use throwing bean bags and teddys too.

The Imaginary Balloon

If I can get my child to hear me, I love using this! I often talk of anger bubbles, like a bottle of fizzy pop that's been shaken when I get angry – I just need to pop my lid and fizz all over. This is a way to release some of that pressure by taking the lid off slowly.

'Anger can really bubble up inside us sometimes, shall we try to blow it away?'

'Can you help me blow up a big balloon?'

(Start blowing up an imaginary balloon – describe its shape and colour. I often choose a mermaid balloon, and giggle when it bumps the ceiling.)

'Here hold this,' – pass an imaginary string, start blowing up a favourite character, and ask your child to complete it. My son used to get tractor balloons, now he chooses dinosaurs.

You can switch this to an imaginary cake and candles – you can pretend it's a relighting candle or that they missed it. The trick is to get them to do a big inhale, and a big controlled exhale.

Using breathing and focusing on something else gives children a chance to slow down their thinking. It switches the nervous system from reactive to more relaxed, and is something I teach all of my busy parents – how to breathe, to calm down and think, or 'meditate in a moment' as I call it.

Snow Globe

Using a snow globe, or a water bottle with glitter in it, can help explain anger to children.

Demonstrate how, if they are angry, it's like shaking the globe and all the snow is swirling and whirling and clouding their vision. As they wait calmly, all of the snow settles and they can clearly see the scene inside.

This works beautifully to discuss what happened once your child has calmed down.

Parent Time-Out

I know I said earlier that time-outs weren't good, however, showing self-directed, own-choice removal from a situation can be really good for the long-term wellbeing of everyone – just resist your inner 13-year-old's need to slam the door on your way out!

When parenting gets too much for me - when I'm not in the right frame of mind to deal with it all fairly or rationally - I need a minute to think.

Recently, I wanted to go to a vegan fair that was quite a drive away. My children were being kids – getting out toys, watching TV, chasing each other round, taking a week to eat breakfast, screaming at each other. There was inaction and movement and noise all around me. They weren't eating their breakfast or putting their shoes on so that we could do something fun together – including buying cake and cheese!

I shouted, lost my cool, and quickly realised that I was in the wrong! (It happens, I am human.) I apologised and said I needed some space to get myself together, so I went to my bedroom and sat on my bed for a while. Eventually, they came to find me, and we discussed my behaviour and how I could have dealt with it better. This gave them the opportunity to reflect on their own behaviour too. And we concluded it was six of one and half a dozen of the other! My desire to go out was time sensitive, and I'd missed the opportunity now, but I could see that all they wanted to do that day was play. That afternoon, we baked and painted, I let go of expectations, and reconnected with them. So what that we missed out on cheese!

I use 'Mummy needs a minute to think about how to deal with this' from time to time. Sometimes, that means asking them to leave me to calm down, to please go upstairs and play with your toys, to not be near me right now as I want to deal with this fairly.

My children will occasionally explain they need time alone to deal with an emotion, and that is self-directed. We have sat close, offering hugs or presence to the three-year-old, while she cried and sobbed and kicked the floor before falling asleep naked on the landing!

We Will Survive

Parenting is tough, but it can be easier if we relax a little and not expect children to be sunny and happy all the time. They will throw big wobblers at times that are inconvenient to us, and that's OK - I'm sure we adults won't be level and even tempered all the time, either. We are learning to parent one day at a time, and they are learning to be themselves one day at a time. Relationships fluctuate, emotions too. Without the ups, we'd never have downs. The triggers for our stresses are adult minded; the triggers for their stresses are child minded. Based in thought, the thoughts will pass as thousands of thoughts pass each day. We are the adult and we know this. Help your children learn it by modelling, apologising, and looking after yourself. A tired stressed out mummy who doesn't eat well, who doesn't sleep well, and who doesn't have time for exercise will not always make the right decisions.

By trying to fix anger, we can make it worse. By ignoring it and pretending it doesn't live at our house, we are making it a bad part of us. By calmly allowing it to pass, we diffuse it – and then learn from it.

When the heat has dispersed, we can talk about the fact that Maisy didn't want to play with him, or why when Mummy said no it was for a reason – and can he now understand why. We don't have to give in to all of our children's wants (perceived needs), we don't always have to put them above our own needs, and we don't have to wrap them in cotton wool and hide the world from them. We just need to be there for them, warts and all.

Let's Reflect

There's no such things as a bad emotion, only ineffective ways of dealing with them.

It's important to let young children be at peace with all of their emotions.

Giving yourself a time-out can be really good for the long-term wellbeing of everyone.

Children deserve to be loved unconditionally, warts and all.

About the Author

Nurse Rachel Devereux was a high-achieving community staff nurse with the NHS. She progressed through the ranks as a health care assistant to achieve a Masters in Long Term Conditions.

When Rachel birthed her children, she birthed the mother inside her. Life suddenly made a lot more sense, but that high achiever burnt out trying to be the perfect mother and the perfect wife and the perfect nurse. Recognising burnout in herself as a working mum, she recognised it in the parents around her. She saw the wilful self-neglect, the negative health behaviours resulting from stress, and decided to take action to help prevent and reverse ill health. Her own recovery gave her the necessary understanding for helping people and, having gone on to train with some of the leading Three Principles Practitioners from around the world, Rachel now has a firm grasp of our innate wellbeing.

Rachel helps others to realise their own strengths in the face of despair. She helps parents become the calm within their child's storm, and she helps to neutralise the negative mind chatter that keeps us stuck in our own storms. Rachel's training with experts in health and parenting, using the Three Principles as defined by Sydney Banks, stands her apart from other coaches as she helps people access their own wisdom and regain the trust in themselves to be self-sufficient and not reliant on others to 'fix' them. We are never broken – we simply think we are! Rachel's simplistic style has the power to allow you to change your whole life, helping you to slow down, relax, and see the trees within the wood.

Connect with Rachel:

Facebook: www.facebook.com/RD.HealthNurseCoach

Instagram: www.instagram.com/healthy_life_coach_rachel

Rachel's book **There Was A Baby: A poem for rainbow children to learn about their siblings who died through miscarriage and stillbirth** is available from Amazon.

Your Teen Knows Best!

By Cai Graham

'Family is not an important thing. It is Everything.'

~ Michael J Fox

'Children should be seen and not heard.' Remember that?

I experienced this a lot as a child. This sentient wasn't meant in a detrimental way – it's just how it was. Children were expected to not question their elders. Why?

Because 'Adults Know Best'.

Children's opinions were less important, and in some instances, things haven't changed much. What I *still* find unsettling is hearing parents say to their children, 'Because I said so,' offering no further explanation.

I bet my bottom dollar you've used this phrase before – I know I have as a parent. But not any longer; I'd never get away with it now.

Let me explain why this antiquated point of view no longer holds much water in today's parenting environment. 'Because I said so' means …

- Do it my way
- I'm running out of ideas

- I'm too busy to explain

It's just rather lazy.

When parents impose (and I do mean impose) their likes and dislikes on their children, they are hampering their child's development. An easy example being food preferences. If a parent dislikes fish, the likelihood is that the child will not be fed much fish. The same applies for beliefs and opinions. Youngsters tend to accept this form of parenting, but teenagers, forging their own way in the world, are less likely to comply.

As your children grow up, you naturally encourage them to:

- Think on their feet
- Develop a mind of their own
- Become independent young adults

(so long as they still do as they're told!)

Teenagers are wired to question their parents authority - and that's as it should be.

'But this is my house, my rules!'

Unsurprisingly, comments like this are greeted with the familiar eye-rolling and door slamming from teenagers. But unchecked, one might start to notice deeper resistance setting in, manifesting as arguments and resentment.

Parents want to protect their child, and to keep them out of trouble. Wanting them to avoid making mistakes is reasonable; after all, kids haven't got the life experiences that parents have.

'Calm seas never made a skilled sailor.'

However, nobody learns without making their own mistakes; and yes, while it's painful to witness, it's a very necessary part of their childhood.

Arguing Doesn't Mean Bad Relationships

A recent study showed that '25% of 16 to 21-year-olds regularly argue with their mothers; whilst 16% row with their fathers.' However, on a more positive note, '67% of those questioned confided in their mums and 50% confided in their fathers.' *(Source : 2011 UK Longitudinal Household Survey, capturing information on the social & economic circumstances of people living in 40,000 UK homes.)*

Now, more than ever, we must communicate effectively with our children as they embark on adulthood. So, it's helpful to consider the following:

1. Lower expectations – nobody has to be perfect.
2. Treat your teen as an equal - surprisingly, this builds respect
3. Allow them to make their own mistakes.
4. Explain your decisions and reasonings behind those decisions.
5. Listen to their opinions.

During your child's development, it's important to understand their hopes and dreams and acknowledge the adult they are becoming. Not only do your teens need the space to grow, they also need your support. Their opinions matter. And why do I say all this?

Because your child knows BEST.

They are the experts in their own lives. They know what interests them. They are forming their own opinions. And, above all, your child knows what's going on in their own head.

We are living in a world where your child is being exposed to cyber-bullying, knife crime, gun violence, gender fluidity, and climate change. Self-harm and anxiety statistics are skyrocketing. It's not the same world that we grew up in; and, therefore, many of our own experiences are now redundant.

We Are Never Too Old to Learn

By being more open-minded and flexible in this ever-changing world, we are better placed to guide and support our children through adolescence. When your child knows that you have their back, rather than being *on* their back, that's when the magic happens.

The teenage brain is a work-in-progress, so expect increased risk taking and questionable decision-making – it's part of the process.

> *'The hardest thing is not talking to someone who you used to talk to you every day.'*

Their brains are re-wiring for independence; and that also means separation. That is totally normal. It is biology. Understandably, there are many changes that parents have to accommodate during their child's growth:

- Emotions fluctuate
- Friends become more influential
- Sleep and behaviour patterns change
- You have less 'authority'
- They stop talking to you

Sometimes, these adjustments can be really hard to deal with.

Oftentimes, parents are aware their child is struggling, and yet it seems impossible to get through to offer help. By the time puberty arrives, you have come to understand your child so well. Any warning signs are easily recognisable:

- Increased irritability and panic
- Reduced energy
- Mood swings & meltdowns
- Withdrawing from friendships.

Rest assured, all this is totally normal. Teenagers are trying so hard to garner their independence that they are often reluctant to admit when they are in need of some support. Many parents are left feeling powerless as to know how to help without being seen as interfering. Let's face it, any self-respecting teenager will retreat when they think that their parent is looking to have a 'meaningful conversation'!

Shut Up and Listen

Parenting can be very unpredictable - the goalposts keep changing. So, what can parents do without appearing needy and desperate?

> 'A child seldom needs a good talking to as a good listening to.'

When your child does eventually want to talk, are you paying attention?

When we feel loved, understood and respected, our confidence and self-esteem rise. We feel able to conquer anything. That's what your child needs to feel, often. How do parents facilitate that? By listening and giving them the space to tell you who they are - what's important to them, what matters to them, what scares them, what excites them. It all starts with listening:

10 Listening Skills

Make eye contact: Done wrong, this makes the conversation feel like an interrogation. Carried out correctly, it shows you are paying attention. Try chatting while cooking, driving or walking the dog. It removes the intensity of talking 'face-to-face'.

Be open-minded: A teen who feels judged will naturally withdraw from the conversation.
Encourage Conversation: Ask open questions, so they have

to say more. There's a difference between, 'Are you alright?' and 'Tell me about how you are feeling,' or 'What went on today?'

Be supportive: You don't have to condone their behaviour, but it's important to offer support. It's easier to manage a tough situation when both parties are working together. Youngsters mess up; yet it's the adult's job to help them make amends and learn from their mistakes.

Be empathic: Being the voice of understanding shows you acknowledge how they feel. Reassure them.

Detach from your feelings: It's often hard to remove your own emotions; but detachment allows you to think with more clarity.

Mind Your Language

The *wrong* communication can result in *mis*-communication. So, when your child does want to talk with you, how do you handle the situation without blowing the opportunity? Sometimes we say things the wrong way unintentionally, leading to more hurt and upset. Practicing language skills can reduce the risk of saying the wrong thing in the heat of the moment.

Try practicing these suggestions:

Remain Calm: Raised voices never get a point across clearly. The recipient is more likely to feel defensive and not heed possibly well-meaning advice.

State your expectations (early on): Words are often open to interpretation. 'Be home early,' means many things!

Avoid threats: Parenting shouldn't really be about controlling the child – whatever their age. Parenting is about managing expectations, setting appropriate boundaries, and offering guidance. Threats are like punishments; they can and will build resentment and anger.

Don't fix things immediately: As tempting as it may be, trying to make everything better benefits no one. But if you want your children to grow into fully functioning young adults, then they learn so much more if they try and figure stuff out for themselves. All this builds resilience and strengthens their own decision-making skills.

Pay attention to the small stuff: The purpose of conversation is to understand and communicate. However, conversation can also deepen connection.

Are your daily interactions meaningful? If not, then building rapport is the next obvious step. This is never more important than in the home.

How Do We Build Rapport?

Rapport builds on the similarities that you have, while also respecting each other's differences.

10% of the communication is down to the words that you use. 90% of everything else.

Teenagers tend to form new and strong opinions very quickly. When these opinions differ from their parents', it's likely to cause friction. Music preferences is a great example.

It's often the first (and safest way) for a child to challenge their previous upbringing and test out what suits them better.

New choices do not have to lead to conflict as it is a natural progression on a child's path to 'grown-up thinking' … but many parents take this transformation as an affront to their previous parenting approach and feel these changes very personally.

A child's individuality is based on the foundation of their family. The family first teaches them, not only about relationships, but about principles and values – which they go on to develop as they negotiate the challenges of daily life.

How do we build rapport when emotions are running high?

Rapport shows us that making better connections is not just about building verbal and listening skills. There are so many other factors at play. It helps to pay attention to the tone of the voices that you can hear and the body language because that's how we can start building better understanding.

Find that common bond: Finding commonality can draw us

together. Start by watching a movie together or enjoying your favourite restaurant meal. You don't have to all like exactly the same things, but doing stuff with one another creates togetherness.

Simply ask their opinion: As the parenting goalposts change, your role is swapping from manager to mentor. It therefore helps to find out what their opinions are and what they believe in. Teenagers need to use parents as a sounding board - to see what it's like to actually voice their own opinions. They are not likely to get it right first time, so allow them the space to develop.

Seek clarification: There is nothing worse than getting the wrong end of the stick. When you make an assumption, you open up the possibility of misunderstanding. Seeking clarification ensures you are both 'talking the same language'.

How to Avoid Overwhelm

Trying to implement these strategies all at once would be a daunting task. Big tasks are often best when broken down into manageable chunks. The following technique is a credible 'first step'. It will turn this 'lack of communication' on its head. It's fast. It's easy to understand. It's unobtrusive – and teenagers love it because (no offence) it gets you off their back!

Just a couple of pointers, however:

- Explain this technique to your children first
- Don't over use it; and, most importantly,
- You have to abide by the rules

Three questions to ask your uncommunicative teen:

Question 1: What's Your Number?

You're looking for an answer on a sliding scale between 1 and 10.
1 = awful, really bad, possibly having suicidal thoughts.
10 = brilliant, on top of the world, there is no need to worry about me.

This offers a quick way of working out how your child is

currently feeling. With regular use, you soon learn your child's 'norm'. Remember that each child is different, so do not compare their numbers.

Question 2: What's Your Word?

Here you are looking for a describing word. Something that expresses how your child is feeling at present. You want a word that paints a picture of their emotions and their feelings.

Examples being: angry, furious, betrayed, embarrassed, stressed, happy, optimistic, hopeful, proud, excited etc.

The more descriptive, the better. Don't accept 'fine'; this doesn't properly describe how they are feeling. This question helps build your child's emotional intelligence. They are able to get in touch with how they are *really* feeling, expanding their emotional vocabulary. Again, it gives you an insight into their frame of mind and how they are currently feeling.

Question Three: Do You Want to Talk?

This is the deal breaker! If your child wants to talk - great! This is progress. If your child does not want to talk … back off! Nine times out of 10 the answer is going to be NO. You have to respect your child's answer. Those are the rules.

What is genius about this is that your child has control, which is what they need right now. Your child has the space to process their stuff at their own pace, without any interference from you. More importantly, the message behind this question says to your child, *'I'm here for you, I've got your back.'*

A word of caution: if and when your child says 'yes' to the question, do not pounce! Gently ask them whether now is the right time to talk. Perhaps they would prefer to go for a walk or a drive? Do not scare them away with your eagerness to talk to them and extract that longed for information. Set the scene so that the two of you can have a calm conversation.

One of the by-products of this exercise is that you will find your child spends less time in their room and more time in the family space. The simple reason being that they know they are not going to be subjected to the Spanish Inquisition.

One mother reported, 'I'm beginning to talk to my child about many other things. I really like the person he is becoming. He's really quite interesting!'

This exercise serves as an excellent early warning system, because you are able to spot mood changes and possible problems earlier; communication opens up naturally over time.

As you spend more quality time with your teenager, you'll start building a deeper connection with them – all of which is instigated by an exercises that asks you to use fewer words! These techniques open the door for you both to have better conversations and, in the long run, build a stronger, more adult relationship.

Let's Reflect

Your child knows best. They know what's going on in their own head.

Develop listening skills. This shows your child that you care and that you value their opinions.

Develop language skills. Talking helps you clarify what you have heard and avoids misunderstandings.

Build rapport. Find the commonality that brings you both together, naturally.

About the Author

From housewife to NLP Master Practitioner & parenting expert, Cai Graham has been in the trenches of parenting and is now on a mission to equip parents and teens with the tools for navigating adolescence.

Cai is a parenting & teen coach, speaker and Amazon #1 bestselling author of *The Teen Toolbox™*. She specialises in supporting families overcoming obstacles - including communication issues, loss and trauma - so that they can enjoy a brighter future.

Cai's mission is to help parents support their children through adolescence, so that together we can build a mentally healthier and happier generation of young people. In creating the Peak Parenting framework and The Teen Toolbox™ series, Cai helps parents reconnect with their children. Her work is about encouraging investment in our children, investment in their future and, ultimately, investment in the next generation.

Connect with Cai:

Website: www.caigraham.com
Email: cai@caigraham.com,
Facebook: @thecaigraham
Instagram: @caigraham
YouTube: www.caigraham.com/YouTube
Podcast: The Parent Toolbox - www.caigraham.com/podcast

Subscribe to Cai's podcast at the link above, and grab her FREE 'Three Questions' download at:

www.caigraham.com/threequestions

Self-Care for Parents and Children

By Jessica Brittani

'Taking care of yourself is an essential part of taking care of others. The healthier the tree, the better the fruit it can offer.'

~ Susan Sutradhar

Self-care has become 'the cool thing to do' recently. Logically, we know that we cannot pour from an empty cup, and that our children will get the best of us when we take better care of ourselves. But how do we learn to take better care of ourselves in a society that tells us the busier we are the 'better' we are, and that self-sacrifice as the ultimate expression of love for our children? And how do we choose our self-care when our family requires so much of our time and attention?

I like to use the term self-love more than self-care. It's the same thing but, for me, life is based around love. So, the most important person we should be giving our love to is ourselves. It sounds more common but the more we learn to love ourselves, the more we are able to express ourselves lovingly to others. One way that we can show ourselves love is through self-care.

Self-care isn't selfish, it's essential. When we take time to care for ourselves, we can:

1. Lower stress levels
2. Feel more energised and revitalised

3. Be better, healthier, calmer parents
4. Teach our children to value their health and wellbeing (my personal favourite)

As Khhyati Ratthod said, 'Real self-care can't be bought, it isn't just spa days and facials. Real self-care is a series of tough decisions – the decision to be more disciplined, to address your recurring toxic thoughts, to prioritise your mental health, and to put your HAPPINESS over your HISTORY.'

It's important to take some time to rest and recover, especially as a parent. Many of us ignore the signs from our body to slow down until it's too late and burnout has already set in, usually showing up in the physical body. We cannot fully support our family and be the person that they need if we are drained. You don't always have to be busy and push yourself so hard. It is okay to pull back and take care of yourself – you owe it to yourself and your children. Those moments of self-care will add purpose, value, energy, and creativity to everything you do, and shine more of *you* in your parenting.

When we feel 'grungy' (negative) feelings, it's usually because we aren't checking in with ourselves and our own needs. As parents, it's easy to put everyone else's needs first while neglecting our own. When we check in and see what we need in that moment, and meet those needs, the grungy feelings go away. This is why self-care (and self-love) is so important. When we give ourselves the care and love that we need, we are able to overcome life's challenges with more ease.

Self-love is a necessity; it is a basic need. It's as important as the air that you breathe. It doesn't matter if you currently feel unworthy of that love just yet, you have to start giving it to yourself now, nonetheless. In time, you'll come to realise just how much you needed it. Love yourself fully as you are (including flaws - those parts that you dislike), and where you are on your journey to becoming your best self. *Focus on all that you are* instead of what you are not.

Make it a daily practise to show yourself kindness, patience, and compassion. Treat yourself like someone you love, like your child. Moment by moment, choose the more loving option. Some days, you'll find it harder to love yourself then others, and that's perfectly okay! Continue to gently love and support yourself in the best way that you can.

What Does Self-Love Look Like?

Many of us didn't learn to love ourselves growing up, so the thought of loving oneself as an adult can feel uncomfortable, impossible, and self-indulgent. However, having a richer experience of life and the world around us, and creating deeper connections with our children, requires us to get into a deeper partnership with self. The more we love ourselves, the more that love ripples to others. The more we model self-love to our children, the easier it is for them to learn it for themselves. Self-love is a truly radical act – it has the power to change the world.

Self-love is keeping promises to ourselves

How does it feel when a friend makes a promise to us and then lets us down? It doesn't feel good. Well, we make and break promises to ourselves all the time! It's so much easier to have a lie-in instead of a workout, or turning on the TV instead of taking those steps towards our goals. It's easy to be comfortable and do what feels safe and familiar. Unconsciously, when you continue to break promises to yourself, you view yourself as unreliable and create a story that you aren't important or worthy of this time for you.

More often than not, when we make a promise to ourselves, it's usually to better ourselves in some way. When I first had the realisation that I wasn't keeping promises to myself, I decided to start flossing. It has taken me many months to build this habit and to finally floss every day. And I am so proud of myself. It is such a small task, yet one that is kind to my body – self-love in action!

Start small and take baby steps towards a promise and goal. You are 1000% worthy of time for *you*. You *are* important. Treat yourself like you would treat your best friend.

Action steps to guide you to keep promises to yourself:

- Write it down
- Make a progress journal
- Start small

Self-love is positive self-talk

What is self-talk? Self-talk is the message we give to ourselves out loud or in our thoughts. These can be positive or negative words. Have you ever caught yourself saying something like, 'I hate how fat I've gotten,' 'I can't leave the house looking like this,' 'I am so stupid! I can't believe I did this!' These are examples of negative self-talk. These words only serve to make us feel worse and, as parents, often (unintentionally) become the voice we speak into our children. They hear every word we say (even when we think they don't) which becomes their subconscious voice passing down those limiting beliefs.

We are constantly 'talking' to ourselves. I have noticed with my own self-talk how critical I can be to myself. When taking my first yoga exam, I had a practise session beforehand and, within two minutes, began crying hysterically. My friend looked up at me and said, 'I hope you aren't this critical to me when I'm practising.' It was such an eye-opening moment. Until that moment, I had no idea how harsh and critical I was being to myself. We all make mistakes. I had to have self-compassion that if I said the wrong thing – IT IS OKAY!

Mistakes help us grow, providing the wisdom, experience, and learning opportunities we would otherwise miss out on. Since that moment, I am extra intentional with my self-talk/thoughts.

Everyone needs praise and approval in life, so why not give it to yourself? This one can be tricky to begin with, but once you create a habit of speaking nicely to yourself, it comes naturally and effortlessly.

Action steps to guide you to speak more positive to yourself:

- Positive affirmations, e.g. 'I am beautiful inside and out.'
- Express gratitude
- Mirror Talk

Self-love is giving yourself space

Giving yourself space to decompress, re-energise and heal is vital. So how do we give ourselves space? Meditate.

April 30th marked two years since my dad's passing. I knew the date was coming up, so I booked myself solid, to stay nice and busy. Well, the overwhelm and anxiety hit and I started noticing those grungy feelings coming up. What I quickly learned (before the day came, thankfully) was: *I needed to be there for myself.*

Time doesn't heal but giving ourselves space - that is how we heal.

Giving ourselves positive space is also important. Recently, I spent several months travelling and living my dream! However, I still encountered up and down moments. Initially, I found this frustrating. I was, after all, living the life I'd worked so hard for - why was I still having down moments? I recognised that, no matter what we are doing in life, there will always be up moments and down moments, and that is okay. Life is about being aware of those positive moments that make your heart happy and those 'up' feelings, no matter how fleeting. I relish those moments now, while also giving myself space for the 'down' moments too.

Action steps to guide you give yourself space:

- Feel your feels

- Journal
- Call a friend
- Meditate
- Express gratitude
- Name your emotions
- Be patient with yourself
- Do things that make your heart happy

Self-love is being your authentic self

What does it even mean to be authentic? To be our authentic self, we are making choices every moment of every day to act, feel, and show our *true* self, rather than a particular side or aspect. It is expressing your whole self genuinely.

Ways to be true to yourself could include: speaking your truth, having boundaries, no longer allowing the desire to be liked to dictate your behaviour, and maintaining alignment between what you feel and need, and what you say and do. There are many tiers of being authentic to ourselves.

Sometimes it can feel uncomfortable or scary to be our whole authentic self. We may fear judgement or feel guilty for what other people in the world are currently experiencing.

> *'Speak your truth, even if your voice shakes'*
> ~ Maggie Kuhn

A great way to practise speaking your truth is recognising and naming how you feel, right now. Literally, right now! Let's try it. Take thirty seconds, take a deep breath, and reflect on how you feel. Notice how you might be carrying your body – are your shoulders or jaw tense? Perhaps you are on auto pilot and just reading. In order to communicate your feelings authentically, you must first have awareness around how you feel.

We do not need to modify our behaviour to be liked. I did this for far too many years. I was always a people pleaser. On the other hand, I constantly had a heavy feeling in my chest and would 'leak' tears because I couldn't keep them pushed down anymore. It took me years to be okay and accept that I am a sensitive person and that I cry … a lot! I cry because I am sad, angry, frustrated, happy, grateful, etc. Any reason to cry, I am probably crying, and that is okay. That is me being true to myself.

What's amazing is that, when we are authentic to ourselves, we stop caring what other people think. When I am true to myself, if someone disapproves of my behaviour, I choose not to have them in my close circle.

I was recently talking to my cousin. She mentioned her struggle to say 'no' to her children. She wants to speak up and say no but is too tired to deal with what could potentially be a tantrum; it's easier to give in and give the boys what they want. Her true desire is to say no. So, in these situations she isn't being authentic or true to herself.

It's also important to recognise our children's need to be authentic and to speak *their* truth. If we are to step into authenticity and model what that looks like to our children, by default we are giving them permission to do the same. This means that there may be aspects of their 'truth' that you, as a parent, may find uncomfortable, especially as they are still learning to find their voice and use it in a constructive way. Of course, guide them and have boundaries, but continue to be the safe space for them to express their truth, no matter how emotionally triggering it may feel at times.

Action steps to guide you to be your authentic yourself:

- Breathing exercises to stay calm, patient, understanding and sympathetic of the child's point of view
- Remind yourself how strong you are to hold your ground
- Positive affirmations, e.g. 'I've got this.'

Self-love is letting out your inner child

What is your inner child?

Children love to play. Play is such an important thing to do when you're a child. Playing is vital to our well-being and is linked to increasing creativity in solving problems, and makes our heart happy. Play has been linked to improvements in mood, alertness, and motivation by increasing our dopamine production, helping to reduce worry and anxiety. Who doesn't like playing?

We all have an inner child within us who wants to play! It *needs* to play. However, as adults, we often disconnect from this part of us and take life (and ourselves) far too seriously.

As parents, this can look like struggling to play with our children, or feeling very self-conscious when it comes to being playful.

We can add play into any part of our lives. I'm literally writing this chapter while listening to music and dancing!

Action steps to guide you to your inner child:

- Write a letter from your inner child to your now self. Use your opposite hand to help take away the logical brain
- Dance
- Use your imagination
- Put a picture of yourself when you were younger and during a difficult time in your life on your night stand or phone background. Send your younger self love whenever you look at it

Self-love is forgiving yourself

> *'You made the best decision you could with the information you had back then.'* ~ David Pogue

As parents, we often look back and feel guilty for how we treated our children! However, guilt is futile if we didn't know any better. And, as the above quote suggests, we did the best we could with the limited information and resources that we had at the time. So, it's time to forgive yourself!

Now that you're a parent and understand what your own parents went through, you may feel guilt for some of your behaviour towards your parents growing up. Again, show yourself some forgiveness and compassion for not knowing any better at the time.

Learn from your mistakes and go forward. I invite you to try this affirmation: 'I forgive myself for judging myself for _____. (Fill in the blank, e.g. for getting sick, for yelling, for not finishing the dishes/laundry, blaming others, not taking self-responsibility, etc.)

Action steps to guide you towards forgiving yourself:

- Practise ho'oponopono (you can find a meditation on my website)
- Check in with yourself, and ask yourself the following

questions:

- What am I blaming myself for?
- What is my inner critic/negative self-talk saying?
- What are the truths?
- What can I do for myself that makes my heart happy? (Celebrate your self-forgiveness)

Self-love is balanced self-care

Before I began writing this chapter, I had a deadline to launch an online membership. I was taking baths once a week, meditating twice a day (morning and night), doing yoga 2-3 times a week, going on long walks, and having dance parties. Yet, I still felt that 'grungy' feeling, no matter how much self-care I was apparently doing. Then I realised – I was barely eating! I was so busy that I forgot to eat, and so overwhelmed that, when I did sit down, I had no appetite.

The point is, self-care is not only one thing – it's like a pie that has so many different slices to eat. We can find a balance to take care of ourselves in every single way, just like we take care of our babies. There are no right or wrong pieces to the pie. Here are a few pieces commonly used:

Physical self-care - This refers to making sure you get enough rest, eat healthy foods, drink enough water, and exercise/movement. More than a 'to do' list or New Year's resolution, these habits help you be at your best each and every day.

Emotional self-care - This involves acknowledging your feelings and working through them. As I mentioned earlier, 'feel your feels'. Sharing your thoughts with others or writing them down can also help.

Spiritual self-care - This type of self-care expands your sense of self in comparison to the rest of the world. Your spiritual self-care may involve regular practises like meditation and prayer. You may also find that being out in nature helps.

Relational self-care – This taps into your sense of social wellbeing. When you're in contact with others who care about you, your obligations are lighter and the challenges you're facing can be put into perspective.

Cognitive self-care - Sadly ignored, this type of self-care refers to your need to continue learning and growing through journaling, reading, or writing gratitude letters to those you are grateful for.

Action steps to guide you to balance self-care:

- Create action plan
- Try using a habit building app

Emergency Self Care Checklist/Ideas

(List of quick short and sweet ideas when you need quick coping skills)

- Mindful 5 senses
- Belly breath
- Gratitude
- Body Scan
- Dance Party
- Journal
- Draw/Paint
- Take a bath
- Loving Kindness Meditation

For a breakdown of all the action steps mentioned

throughout the chapter go to:

www.calmandcolorful.com/selfcare

Let's Reflect

Self-care isn't selfish, it's essential.

As a parent, it's important to make time (and space) to recharge your batteries! *Everybody* benefits.

Start small and take baby steps towards a goal. You are 1000% worthy of time for *you*. You *are* important. Treat yourself like you would treat your best friend.

Connect with your inner child and play more. Play is vital to our well-being and has been linked to improvements in mood, alertness, and motivation by increasing our dopamine production, helping to reduce worry and anxiety.

Forgive yourself and show self-compassion for the mistakes you made when you didn't know better, learn from those mistakes and move forward.

About the Author

Jessica Brittani is an author, speaker, mindfulness mentor and creator of Calm & Colorful. Growing up she struggled with minimal self-worth which led to a life with depression and anxiety. Her mission is to guide children, families and teachers to know their self-worth and hopefully prevent feelings of depression or anxiety. She wants children to feel confident that they have the life skills toolbox to face challenges throughout life and in the home and/or classrooms. Jessica is also creating an interactive colouring book series that teaches different coping skills. She travels full time to do workshops at schools and events.

Connect with Jessica:

Website: www.calmandcolourful.com
www.calmandcolorful.com

Email: Jessica@calmandcolorful.com

Facebook: @calmandcolorful

Instagram: @calmandcolorful

For weekly mindfulness tips, text MINDFUL to 474747

www.ingramcontent.com/pod-product-compliance
Lightning Source LLC
Chambersburg PA
CBHW071728080526
44588CB00013B/1939